Native American Herb

Encyclopedia + Dispensatory + Remedies + Recipes

MW01396847

Table of Contents

BOOK 1:

Native American Herbs

About the Author

Maya Davis was born on the Crow Creek Indian Reservation (South Dakota)in 1979.

She grew up in close contact with the ancient culture of Native Americans and had the opportunity to learn about medicinal plants directly from her grandfather, shaman, and healer of the tribe.

From a young age, Maya understood how valuable her ancestors' knowledge was and decided that she would spread the culture of herbalism throughout the country.

At the age of 18, she moved to Chicago, where she successfully attended the College of Naturopathy and Dietetics, acquiring the necessary certifications to practice as a naturopath.

Currently, Maya . lives in South Dakota, where she runs a nutritional consulting practice, making extensive use of medicinal plants.

In her free time, she enjoys walking in nature and looking for medicinal plants to add to her cultivation.

Her mission is to spread the Native American culture and show that it is possible to minimize the use of industrial medicines thanks to a good knowledge of herbs.

Introduction

For thousands of years, man has used alternative medicine to cure illnesses, fight viruses, and find solutions to stubborn diseases. These methods have been carefully developed, researched, and preserved to be useful for generations to come. Then came modern civilization and its complexity that brought us further and further from nature. Everything changed, and much of the old wisdom was forgotten.

Native American medicine used to be an essential part of human existence in Northern America. It was vital for the people as it ensured their health and ability to fight off infections. Then came modern medicine, and people came to disdain these natural remedies that existed and were effective long ago. Instead of free and natural treatments provided by the earth, the desire to make huge profits from people's illnesses has now become the primary impetus behind our medical system.

In recent years, people are beginning to investigate if humans can benefit from the lifestyle of people who existed hundreds and even thousands of years ago. Based on research, these people had fewer medical problems than what we have today and were able to have good health with very few resources.

Did these Native American people know what we do not know now? What is it that we can learn from them? Do they have the answers to some of the most dangerous health problems that we have today, including cancer, Ebola, and HIV/AIDS?

Native Americans understood the interconnected nature of all life and the truth that a human's well-being depended on the mind, body, and spirit being in harmony. An imbalance in any one of the three and illness results. Through their close connection to the natural world, these ancient people discovered that certain plants could heal specific imbalances in the human body.

Through their collective learning, Native Americans cataloged over 500 different plants and their medicinal uses. What makes this knowledge even more impressive is that this was all done through oral tradition as their knowledge was not written down until modern times.

Despite all of the knowledge and technology at our disposal, modern medicine has severe limitations. If it didn't, we would not be spending billions every year treating illnesses and diseases far more prevalent now than in the past.
Perhaps what modern medicine is missing is a more holistic, nature-based way of approaching health and healing.

In this book, you will learn how to look for and find the perfect Native American medicines. You will receive guidance on working with skilled professionals and the benefits you will derive from using a treatment that is in harmony with nature. You will also learn how using native medicine can help reduce the cost of your medical expenses.
The world of Native American herbal medicine is vast and deeply enriching for those who take the time to explore its treasures.
You may enjoy your exploration and, with the help of this book, gain the knowledge needed to heal yourself.

Chapter 1: - First Things First

In this chapter, we will be discussing wildcrafting, growing, and storage of herbs for herbalism.

Wild Crafting

Wildcrafting is probably the most ancient activity men have ever done. It consists of harvesting plants from the wild for food or medicinal purposes. When done sustainably, this is a win-win for both men and plants: men can receive food or medicinal herbs from nature, and in exchange, they take care of the surrounding environment by taking only what is necessary, replanting plants and seeds, removing dead branches to help the plant grow faster and more robust.

Win-Win Wildcrafting

There are techniques and gathering methods that allow the plant and the surrounding environment to benefit from the harvesting. This is important to minimize the impact we have on our planet and ensure that we have access to nature's benefits for many generations to come. Below some of the most used techniques to adopt in the different situations:

- ❖ Shrubby plant: when cutting a branch or a stem, cut above a leaf node to encourage the plant to grow more. Cut at a 45° angle about 6mm above the node. In case you have a plant with opposite leaves, cut straight across.

- ❖ Replant root crowns whenever you can.

- ❖ Harvest roots only during fall. This season, leaves tend to die, and all the nutrients tend to fall back to the roots.

- ❖ Harvest branches that are already broken but still attached to the plant. This will give you the parts you need and set the plant free from a possible source of infection and disease. Be sure to leave a flat surface.

- ❖ When harvesting branches, make a two-inch deep cut under it before sawing from the top. This will ensure that you do not strip the bark at the end of the cut when the branch falls to the ground in the latter part of the cut.

Rules for Ethical Wildcrafting

The Rocky Mountains Herbalist's Coalition, from Colorado, selected a set of rules to live by when wildcrafting. These rules may seem obvious and common sense, but if followed religiously, it will assure that everyone would benefit from the local flora for generations.

1. Never pick endangered species.
2. Before harvesting, be sure of the plant identification.
3. Ask permission and thank the plants.
4. Leave mature plants which stay in a higher position untouched so they can indeed repopulate the picking zone with the down-slope rolling of seeds.
5. Gather only from abundant stands and no more than 10% of the plant.

How to select the site for wildcrafting

- ❖ Obtain permission from your local authority with a regular license to pick plants.
- ❖ Follow the guidelines of your local authority of where to pick, and what zones to avoid.
- ❖ Stay far away from pollution sources: Roadsides, Electric wires, and farms or gardens that may use chemical fertilizers. Be sure to be upwind or upstream from these areas.
- ❖ Do not pick from a fragile environment.

When to pick

- **Flowers:** Pick them at the beginning of the blooming, possibly during a complete moon phase, between 6 and 10 a.m.

- **Leaf:** pick them before the flowering phase of the plant between 6 and 10 a.m.

- **Roots picking:** to be done after the seeding phase of the plant during the new moon, and early in the morning to avoid deep dirt to dry. For plants with a biannual living cycle, harvest during the autumn of the second year.

- **Barks:** Pick during spring, in the three-quarter waning moon, and never strip the whole tree. Be sure to leave the healthiest plants untouched. If you deny branches to avoid branches too near to the ground to avoid fungal rot on the plant. Pick the inner bark (cambium) and be sure to adopt pollarding techniques for the short branches and coppicing for low stumps.

- **Pitch and Sap:** the favorite season for harvesting is winter.

- **Seeds and Fruits**: harvest when mature according to the natural rhythm of the plant.

How to manage your picking sites

- Do not wear hard-soled shoes, to avoid damages to the ground

- Be aware of the plant's proper lifecycle. Be sure not to harvest the same spot year after year. Observe the picking spot and evaluate through comparative pictures if your impact on the zone is too much. Eventually, avoid the harvesting for a year or two.

- ❖ Provide food to the remaining plants. I use Native American traditional cornmeal, which is handy, but your organic waste such as an apple peel will also do the job.

- ❖ Treat the spot as it would be your garden: tend to it, remove weeds, and make manual pollination if needed.

- ❖ Use appropriate wildcrafting techniques and tools described in this chapter to be sure to cause minimal damage to the area.

- ❖ Digging to find medical roots may cause damages and erosion to the ground. Be sure to cover the holes, and to replace the foliage and dirt on the digging spot.

- ❖ If you are harvesting leaves or flowers, do not eradicate the whole plant.

Wildcrafting Ritual

The picking was one of the most critical phases for the Native American healers. It was the most spiritual and intense part for sure, where you connect with mother nature and you engage with the deities who inhabit the world.

Phyllis Hogan, the founder of the Arizona Ethnobotanical Research Association, is a skilled herbalist. During her forty years of experience in the field, she worked with many Native American tribes (especially **Navajo and Hopi**) and she adopted their gathering rituals:

- ❖ Be sure to wear nice clothes and jewelry as a sign of worthiness in the deity's eyes.

- ❖ You always pick early in the morning. You begin by burning a juniper twig, then collect the soot and smudge some of it in a vertical line in the middle of your forehead while praying to the sun

- Once you find the plant you want to collect, you tell it your name and offer cornmeal to the picking spot.
- Select a plant in the immediate proximity of the one you want to pick and ask permission to pick the surrounding plants explaining that you want to use them for healing purposes. Then you wait for approval.

- It may happen in various forms: a blowing of the wind, the rustling of leaves, or just a feeling. If you do not receive permission, you do not pick.

- Once you receive permission, give cornmeal offerings to the four directions (starting from the east and working clockwise), the middle, and place a pinch of cornmeal on your head. This is a vital sign of connection to the spiritual world.

- **IMPORTANT:** Do not pick the plant you asked permission for. It is your emissary in the plant world. If a plant resists picking, then don't force it. Pick only the plants that come out quickly.

- Never take more than you need; pick 10% of the plant maximum.

- Place what you pick on a clean linen or cotton sheet. Be sure to align all the plants in the same direction and do not mix the species. Place some other cornmeal in the sheet and welcome the plants openhearted. Tell them again why you picked them and why they are needed.

- Do not process them immediately. When you come back home, remove them from the sheet, line them on a table and let them rest for another day. Thank them again before processing.

Wildcrafting Essentials

The right tool for the job. This is an essential concept to understand in any crafting activity, from woodworking to cooking.

When you have the right tool, you work faster and better. You are less exposed to accidental cuts or wounds and, more important, you create fewer damages to the environment and the plants by making clean cuts or more surgical diggings.

Below you can find a list of the essentials you need to start wildcrafting in safety and with ease:

- **A Plant Identification Handbook:** - This is probably an essential tool you need. Clear identification of a plant will tell you if it is edible or poisonous if it is endangered or not and the parts to pick for medicinal or food purposes.

- **Scissors, Clippers, and a sharp Knife**: - Scissors and clippers are valuable tools. They allow clean cuts and minimize the damages to the plant. My advice is to invest and buy good quality tools because they will allow you to make clean cuts with less effort and minimize the possibility of accidentally cutting yourself (even with more hard plants or roots like Echinacea). Ultimately, they will make the job easy and will endure for decades.

Another valuable tool is a sharp knife that will allow you to make an accurate 45° cut on the plant that scissors and clippers can't do.

- **Gloves:** - Essential tools when you deal with thorny and stinging plants and using a knife to protect your hands.

- **Trowel and Folding Shov**el: - These two are unevaluable when digging roots. The scoop will be enough for most roots, but for deeper ones, it is necessary to have in your backpack a folding shovel. They come in every size and cost and, when folded they do not occupy much space.

- **Saw:-** This one is essential when harvesting branches for obvious reasons. It will make clean cuts in the trunk and the tree will be less exposed to diseases and infection

- **Paper Bags and Clean Linen Sheets:** - Although Native American traditions allow only clean sheets to store the plants from the picking place to your home, brown paper bags are a good substitute. The primary function they must have is to absorb moisture and facilitate transpiration of the herbs. Plastic bags are to be avoided at all costs because they encourage mold formation.

Becoming an Experienced Wild Crafter

Only time will give you the tools to know your way with the plants and the environment in your surroundings or pick spots. Of course, there are some tips to speed up the process:

- Observation: take your time with the plants. Look at them with curiosity, and use your nose and touch as well as your eyes. You will begin to notice new things even in the most common plant how it changes from season to season and from year to year in some cases.

- Take notes: whenever you identify a plant, notice where it lives, its neighbor plants, the insects you found. You will understand the patterns and quickly you will know where to look to find the plant you need in no time.

- Keep a sketchbook: even if you are not Leonardo Da Vinci and barely know what a pencil is, I encourage you to keep a sketchbook of the plants you identify. It will help you take the habit of deep and careful observation of the plants.

- Build your herbarium by preserving flowers, leaves, and buds in the middle of a book for some time to make it dry. Then stick it in a notebook.

- Take photos: today technology makes this task more accessible than when I started wildcrafting. You can easily take a picture with your phone and write notes on it.

Safe Wildcrafting Rules

Be sure to follow these simple rules when wildcrafting. It will ensure that you get your feet wet in the safest way possible in this fascinating world. In time, you will develop confidence and knowledge with your environment and you will know what to pick and what to leave:

- Identify the plant before harvesting. There are plenty of poisonous plants that look precisely like medical ones.
- If you have some doubt, do not harvest. Take a picture and check while at home or with your local Extension Office.
- Do not "taste test" plants you do not know.
- Be sure to know the endangered plants in your surroundings.
- Attain to the 10% rule: only harvest the 10% or less of what you find, to be sure not to damage the environment.
- Never harvest near urban environments such as high-tension trellis, or roadsides, or railways.
- Caution: you could be allergic or intolerant to some plant and you don't even know. When you try a new plant, be sure to take small amounts and try only one new plant at a time.
- Keep your eyes open: even if wildcrafting may seem like hiking, it is more different from that. There are many hidden dangers when you go deep into thc woods such as thorns, stinging plants, or holes in the ground that can make you sprain your ankle.

- **Avoid plants with white sap:** this is a big red flag indicating that the plant is poisonous.

- **Flowers in umbels**: Be careful with this one. Many curative plants such as yarrow form flowers in an umbel, but many poisonous look alikes do that. Be 100% sure of what you are picking.

- Exercise additional caution with mushrooms; they could be highly poisonous.

- Many herbs look like mint but they do not smell or taste minty. Many inexperienced wildcrafters have been in trouble by eating poisonous look-alikes.

- If you see an animal eating a specific herb, this is not a sign that the herb is edible. Some animals have developed tolerance to some poisonous plants.

Free Apps for Plant Recognition

Today technology makes the job easier than when I began. There are plenty of websites and apps on the internet that will help you identify the various plants you will encounter.
Below my favorite free apps:

- **Like That Garden**: You can upload your picture and give you immediate recognition of the plant. Recognition is not always 100% reliable and works better with flowering plants, so use your own judgment

- **Leafsnap:** You can upload the picture of the leaf and it will give you immediate recognition of the plant. The picture must be taken on a white background, and this can be impractical

- **ID Weeds:** Developed by the University of Missouri. It will recognize the plant after the input of some attributes. Less practical than the two above but more reliable. You can also check from their pictures database.

- **Vtree:** Developed by Virginia Tech, it gives you a list of plants available in your surroundings by acquiring your GPS position. It also provides plant pictures and descriptions.

- **About Herbs:** it is a database of herbs and plants with pictures, descriptions, and simple medical preparations. My advice is to use it in combination with one of the other apps listed above.

1. **Aerial or above ground constituents:** 6 a.m. - 10 a.m. In the morning, before they are wilting in the sun. Some are better when harvesting leaves only before flowering. You should be able to see the bud's color by only choosing most flowers until they begin to bloom. The standard moon cycle for gathering aerial pieces is before or after the full moon.

2. **Roots:** early in the morning or before sunrise harvest after seeding, if necessary. Biennials: harvest in the fall of the first year or season of the second year. A traditional time is a new moon.

3. **Barks:** Harvest during spring or fall. Don't necessarily strip. Grab a whole crop. Tree thinning is appropriate in dense cities, but the healthiest looking trees refuse to leave. If you take only from the tiny leaves, be careful to make the tree susceptible to fungal rot. For pollarding, the inner bark, or cambium, is the most involved bark among many, leaving small trunks and low stumps for copping. This will have continuous production. Three-quarters of the waning light is the traditional bark method.

4. **Saps and Pitches:** Harvest in late winter or early spring.

5. **Crop and Fruit:** Harvest with some differences when mature, such as bananas, unripe pods of scarlet beans, etc.

1. Dry most plants; stop wire screens and newspaper printing in shaded, well-ventilated regions—analysis into which plants in the sundry better.

2. Don't wash the trees or bulbs. To clean off rodents and dust, shake them. Where quantities are appropriate, attach bundles at the stems' base with diameters of 1 1/2 inches or less. On walls, they may even be loosely scattered to dry.

3. Barks: Peel the exterior bark off if necessary. Here it is named flipping.

4. Roots: Stretch them out or circle. Rinsing can usually not remove soil particles. A pressure hose is sometimes necessary, as well as hand brushing, especially with clay. Cut lengthwise for long, heavy roots without aromatic properties.

5. Both plant elements, when delicate, are dry. In the lower portion, pinch the hanging trees. Break a broad specimen root in half to see if the heart is dry.

1. Stop heat that is light and excessive and might kill aromatic properties and other important constituents. Food grade plastic bags or fiber barrels or other containers that emit oxygen and moisture are suitable to retain consistency and potency as long as possible while they are scorched.

2. Mark with place and dates.

3. Broken or crushed herbs lose their worth more easily than uncut herbs, which are complete.

An infusion is made by immersing an herb in either cold or hot (not boiling) water. The stream, not drinking water, can be the purest you can find. It is safer to provide water from rainfall, good wells or streams, or bottled water. Herbs with potent volatile oils are better infused in cold water (those with an unmistakable scent like essential oil or perfume). In warm water, some herbs perform well.

Depending on the plant, they can be left for some time, from fifteen minutes to overnight, so that the water will consume the plant's essential elements. For the production of infusions and decoctions, glass or earthenware vessels are outstanding. As they won't crack from fire, quart or pint canning jars are fine, and the screw cap prevents the nutrients from floating away in the steam.

Herbalism, which many call phytotherapy, is the use of plants for healing and the maintenance of good health. It is the oldest known medical practice. Before doctors could employ synthetic prescription drugs, they used what they had at hand: plants. It is, in fact, the most widely used form of medicine on the planet. More than 80 percent of the world's population employ it even today.

Perhaps the primary tenet of herbalism that separates it from conventional Western medicine is its holistic nature. Unlike pharmaceuticals, which use isolated compounds from the plants, herbalism employs the entire plant. This is vital since herbalists believe that the substances of the herb are naturally balanced. Using them in that state only encourages healing of the body, mind, and spirit.

As those who practice this tradition, the herbalist or herbal therapist are called, focus on individual therapy. When recommending herbs and treatments, the goal is to incorporate all aspects of the person's life, including mental, emotional, spiritual realms, and the social and environmental areas.

Good health, according to the herbal tradition, is more than merely the absence of disease. It is the existence of a positive state of wellbeing. Herbalism advocates and strives for the promotion of health, indeed. But in contrast to conventional medicine, its goal is to prevent the disease in the first place.

To this end, the herbal healer and the person seeking healing are active partners in the endeavor. The herbalist provides his "patient" with the tools to spark his body's innate ability to heal itself. Unlike conventional medicine, where a patient waits to be treated and cured by the physician, herbalism places the role of healing directly in the individual's hands.

Herbal medicine is misunderstood by many because it blurs the line between foods and drugs. Of course, this is why so many of us are interested in it. And this is why the modern medical community – especially the FDA – doesn't quite know what to do with it.

The FDA – the Food and Drug Administration – is tasked with ensuring all medicines meet stringent safety requirements. Part of that process is the reviewing of massive amounts of research and reviews of human trials of the drug or vaccine.

Herbs escape this intense scrutiny. And so, the FDA has no record of clinical research on them, no human scientific trials, and no way to proclaim them. Unlike what some in the medical community may tell you, that doesn't mean the use of herbs is unsafe. There may not be clinical evidence of its effectiveness, but there is abundant anecdotal evidence.

And here's a quirk in the system. If tests were done on a particular herb, and the FDA would sanction its use, it would immediately be classified as a drug. When someone warns you about herbal use due to no FDA sanction, remember this.

Herbal healing predates the FDA and modern medicine by literal eons. It is, without a doubt, the oldest healing practice on the planet; its use dating back to thousands of years. The use of plants for medicinal purposes is far older than recorded history. Archeologists have discovered the use of plants for this purpose as far back as the Paleolithic age, about 60,000 years ago. (Curiously, humans weren't the first to discover this practice. It seems that other primates also used herbs to treat their illnesses.)

Every culture has its system based on its cultural mores and the plants available in the region.

Ayurvedic Medicine

One of the most well-known herbal systems – and one of the oldest-is India, called Ayurveda. Some believe the use of this particular system of healing began as early as 4,000 BC. The basis of this knowledge is in no small part based on the earliest Sanskrit texts, including the Rig Veda and the Atharva Veda.

Nearly 20 percent of the population of the Indian subcontinent uses some form of this system of medicine that emphasizes the personalization of treatment. Deepak Chopra is its most recognized proponent. A trained medical doctor, he also advocates for the natural, holistic healing of Ayurveda.

Chinese Herbalism

China's traditional system of medicine is also familiar to many and used far outside the boundaries of that country. It has given westerners acupuncture and acupressure. In addition, though, the Chinese have developed a sophisticated system of herbs. The herbs are but a part of what is called Traditional Chinese Medicine. The Chinese, just like the Native Americans, believe that healing an illness is a holistic endeavor. Ailments are a sign your body is out of balance. Traditional Chinese Medicine views the balance of life as two opposing energy forces, the yin and the yang.

Western Herbalism

There is an herbal healing tradition in the Western Hemisphere as well, even though allopathic medicine has tried to reduce it to second-class status and seems at times to try to discredit. It. The ancient Greeks and Romans relied on herbs.

The schism in western medicine of modern medicine and herbal healing may have first begun with Hippocrates. You no doubt have heard of the Hippocratic oath doctors take, but his influence goes beyond that.

He is credited with the authorship of a text called Hippocratic Corpus, which includes herbal recipes and remedies. Inside the pages of this text, there are countless herbs not only native to Greece but also from other geographical areas. It is a complete compendium.

While the information is nearly identical to what religious healers were using at the time, there is one big difference. Hippocrates didn't include the ceremonies and rituals that accompanied those remedies. This omission reveals the logic and the reason with which he approached his vocation.

Herbalism of the Middle Ages

The primary source of all medical knowledge in Europe during the middle ages resided within the Benedictine monasteries. It's been noted that most of the herbal knowledge they possessed was passed down to them from the Greeks and Romans. In turn, the monks laboriously copied these herbs and their uses so as not to lose them. The abbeys naturally became the repositories of medical knowledge. Their gardens, in addition, grew the plants used in the remedies.

But that doesn't mean that the common man didn't practice herbal healing. As we have come to call it, Folk medicine continued unabated both in the home and in the villages. Because of this, you could find either local or itinerant herbalists. The term used to describe these individuals was wise man or woman. They prescribed the remedies, which included spells, advice, and what was thought to be divine insight.

One of the most famous wise women was Hildegard of Bingen. A 12th-century Benedictine nun, she composed the legendary medical text Causae et Curae. Hildegard was a remarkable woman whose faith in natural healing arose from her faith in the Scripture. In this, her beliefs are similar to that of the Native Americans. Her practice was a natural product in the knowledge that humanity as a spiritual creation is not solely bound by natural laws but also a high spiritual law. Today, you can find modern European herbalists who still use many of her remedies.

All the other medical practices that have followed owe a debt of gratitude to the study and use of herbs.

The term herbalism encompasses more than just the use of plants for healing. Many contemporary herbalists practice other approaches to holistic healing, not unlike the Native Americans. Some of their techniques include detoxification, hydrating the body, exercise, and getting outdoors frequently.

The core concept that drives all herbal practice is the belief in the healing power of plants and the corollary love of nature and respect for the environment.

High-quality herbs are high-quality herbs, regardless of their source. Where you live, that might be a local health food store, a small local farm, or even your neighbor's garden. You may even have an herb shop in your town. You might be surprised to find that your grocery store has good-quality herbs, too, especially those frequently sold as produce. Or you may live somewhere with limited access to herbs, in which case you should find a reputable online retailer.

You'll also find that the price of herbs can vary greatly, depending on where you purchase them. Cheaper is not usually better! Local small producers often have to charge more for their spices and herbal products, but the quality is often much higher.

Experiment with small batches first, so you learn which producers have the best quality; that will help you know whether it's worth the money.

There are a few things to keep in mind when sourcing herbs: soil quality, growing practices, and how the herbs are dried or processed.

If the soil where the herbs are grown is contaminated with heavy metals or other pollution, this is likely to be in the plant matter. It's important to know where the herbs were produced, so you can determine whether the soil was clean. This can be a problem for herbs grown anywhere, but especially those grown in places that don't have regulations about soil pollution. Some larger herb retailers, such as Mountain Rose Herbs, test their herbs to ensure they are free of soil-based contamination.

You might be disinclined to purchase herbs grown in urban farms, but don't write them off: Talk to the producers and ask about their soil. Most urban farms bring in clean soil and use water filtration to make sure their product is safe.

Growing practices are also essential. How were insects managed? What kind of fertilizer was used? Were the herbs grown in a greenhouse or outdoors? Were they grown hydroponically or in soil? All these things have pros and cons, but the bottom line is the result: If the herbs have vibrant color and intense aromas and flavors, then the quality is good.

The drying and processing step can be tricky, too: High-quality herbs can be ruined if they're dried at too high a temperature or stored improperly. You'll know this is the case if there is significant browning in the dried herbs. This is the same browning you would see on a living plant with a brown, dried leaf—it looks un-vital. Let's use St. John's wort as an example: This plant should have some brown when it's dried, but its brown color is deep-red mahogany. That's very different from the brown-black color of basil leaves that have gone bad in your refrigerator. The latter is the one to avoid.

The bottom line is, know who you're buying your herbs from. Ask about their growing practices, about the soil and water, and their processing practices. Not only does this help you make good choices, but it also helps build community between the people who grow our herbs (and food) and those of us who consume them. When we understand more about where our spices come from, we value them, our farmers, and our environment more.

The German Swiss physicist & alchemist Paracelsus and the herbalist, physician, and astrologer Nicholas Culpepper developed positions in botanical plant pharmacy, mathematics, alchemy, and astrology in the 16th and 17th centuries. While in today's legitimized occupations, the naturopathic elements of botany and mathematics have been added, astrology and alchemy appear to others merely superstition. But to build a comprehensive method of studying, understanding, and utilizing plant medicine in conflicting ways, this mixture of studies is required. Scientific science has allowed us today to investigate herbs, their properties, and how they act as natural remedies as they are used. Herbal treatments have been checked and validated time and again to produce the same results. Several herbs have been extensively researched, and there is no doubt that they are robust and healthy and have calming properties. Herbal science and regulation are hot topics, and I'm not big on these topics in my job. Therefore, the study will serve to further the use of plant medicines and educate and raise knowledge of herbs' medicinal properties. I deal for the general public, and my herb shop is visited every day by a wide variety of individuals, from many who know little about herbs to professionally qualified herbalists. Every entity needs scientific knowledge of how plants function within the body, and they are suspicious of natural therapies without this. Perhaps further study will open doors for those who, by traditional approaches, are less capable of learning about herbs. It is vital to bear in mind that not all experiments are precise.

Nonetheless, search for details on every analysis you read. Why has the examination been taken? On one part of the plant or the whole item, was the appraisal done? Will the researcher make or sell a product appropriate to the examination that is advertised? This understanding will offer helpful advice about whether, depending on the objectives, the study is factual or subjective. If you wish to support your herbal study interests, we suggest the American Botanical Council (abc.herbalgram.org) & the work of its chairman, the herbalist Mark Blumenthal.

Essential Tools

It doesn't take fancy equipment or rare, expensive ingredients to make high-quality herbal preparations. Most of what you'll need is probably already in your kitchen.

Mason jars. These are the herbalist's best friends. Because they're made of heat-resistant glass, you can pour boiling water right into them to make tea. They're also handy for making tinctures, storing herbs, and more. Quart- and pint-size jars are the most versatile, though for storing dry herbs, you may want more giant pots. Many store-bought foods (sauerkraut, salsa, etc.) come in mason jars—just hand wash or run them through the dishwasher and dry to reuse them.

Wire mesh filters. For straining the tea or pressing out tinctures, you'll want filters of various sizes. Start with a few single-mug strainers for making one cup of tea at a time, as well as a more giant, bowl-size sieve for filtering more significant amounts of herb-infused liquids.

Cheesecloth. This is handy not only for straining and squeezing herbs you've infused into liquid but also for wrapping the herbs in a poultice.

Measuring cups and spoons. Cup, tablespoon, and teaspoon measures are all helpful, as well as some graduated measuring cups with pour spouts, which allow you to measure down to a quarter ounce.

Funnels. A set of small horns is beneficial for getting tinctures and other liquids into bottles with small openings.

Bottles. For storing tinctures long term, amber or blue glass bottles are best. The "Boston round" type is a favorite for potions and other liquid remedies, but any shape will do. Get in the habit of saving and reusing any colored glass bottles you come across—some kombucha brands come in amber glass, for instance.

One- and two-fluid-ounce bottles are most convenient for dose bottles, while storage bottles are usually 4 to 12 fluid ounces. For storage, use plain bottle caps, but you'll need dropper tops for dose bottles.

Labels. Label your remedies as soon as you make them. Address labels are sufficient for most purposes—even a bit of masking tape will do in a pinch.

Blender. A standard kitchen blender will serve just fine for mixing lotions, breaking down bulky fresh plant matter, and other purposes.

Cultivating your herbs at home is an enjoyable way to taste fresh flavors all year long. And as the weather starts becoming more relaxed and the days get shorter, there's just one thing that means: harvest season.

There are a few things you can keep in mind when cultivating plants, no matter what herb you're picking. Here's a realistic tip:

- Just pick herbs when they're dry. It is advisable to reap after the morning dew has gone or at night.
- Just before the opening of the buds, should you harvest culinary herbs? Be sure to pinch several buds before they open, since after they flower, all the plant's energy goes into developing blooms, and then the tasty leaves do not grow well.
- Harvest the seeds until they turn from green to brown. The seeds have to be fragile, dry, and crushable, not brown, but brown.
- Be gentle. Handle them carefully to stop bruising your precious crop when harvesting, as fresh herbs are fragile, so.

Sustainable Foraging Recommendations

<u>1. The abundant plants with a broad, scattered population are forage only.</u>

Not extracting a plant and the threats it may pose from commercial demand or loss of habitat after assessing the population. E.g., a plant may be geographically abundant, but if there is a universal request, it may quickly disappear, with overharvesting decimating the population.

<u>2. Favor for non-native harvesting species.</u>

If the herb is native and connected to local food chains or is a deserter from another location, it is among the first things we remember when choosing which herbs to eat. Through competing with them for natural resources, nonnatives relocate native animals. With the same balances and checks that wild plants have encountered, these resourceful plants have not grown nearby, and so they often thrive. This brands them as primary forage for us humans, mainly because they remain close to places we live, thriving in neighborhoods, gardens, fields, & the like. Non-natives include Rosa multiflora (multiflora rose), Lonicera japonica (Japanese honeysuckle), Albizia julibrissin (Mimosa), Arctium minus (burdock), and several species of raspberry and blackberry are some of our most popular wild feeble medicinal items in the United States (southeast) (Rubus spp).

3. Tend the gaps "in-between."

Wild weeds will naturally arise & make themselves at home with those of you who cultivate a greenhouse and cohabit comfortably with developed vegetables and herbs. You can use plenty of techniques to make them play fair, and you can still collect more medication and food from your greenhouse as an opportunity to serve as a botanical referee! This is the bounty that develops between the medicines and vegetables you have not created yet, that you still have to reap. Frank Cook, a plant friend who died, used to teach in classes that in the form of useful opportunistic plants, more than half of the abundance of a garden may be found in the "in-between." People worldwide profit from this vast resource, casually "cultivating" weeds in the regions in between.

Let us take the quarters of the lamb as an example of this form of useful-weed-&-planted-crop-polyculture. More protein, beta-carotene, vitamin C, zinc, and calcium than cultivated spinach are given by lamb parts, often called wild spinach. Why will you root out such a strong plant that does not need special treatment or protection from pests to make way for less stable crops and more difficult to develop?

It would help if you left the wild spinach in the field between the newly planted vegetables and the herbal crops. The vegetables fill up after planting the wild spinach for a few weeks or a month, and then you can take out the lamb quarters and use them as mulch for the cultivated crops. Because it makes its way into the greenhouse, wild spinach needs little planting and is relatively disease-free and insect-free.

4. Be a steward purely.

And when you pick sufficiently (possibly pesky) species, adhere to a code of ethics. You deal for, after all, honest, breathing animals. Take what you need, leave the beauty of the wake (leave no trace) and make a bid before you go, to make a poem, a little water, hair, a handful of grain. An offering demands a sense of appreciation, reciprocity, and respect. If you are more science-minded, you might take a minute to consciously relax, meditating on the interchange of the exchange of plant-human oxygen, cellular respiration, & photosynthesis. At first, you can sound ridiculous, but give yourself the chance to be shocked. This is how the ancient plant-human dance of friendly friendship, touch, & love influences us.

Be very careful not to overharvest if the plant you are harvesting is organic, so you have already assessed that it is plentiful enough to produce. If you are picking a multi-stem herbaceous plant, cut out a stem or two from each plant. Scatter the crop around a wider field and ensure you leave plants with enough flowers and fruit to reproduce. Replant the root crown while you are extracting roots or take only part of the root system of each plant. Be careful to cut back the aboveground portions while digging up roots so that the plant does not get saturated by water with a root structure that no longer suits its aboveground growth. For resistant weeds with global dispersion, Ses' regenerative methods do not even need to be pursued.

5. Harvesting in situations where you realize that no one has applied herbicide.

Since the surrounding soil is typically polluted with lead, herbicides, and other toxins, there should be no plants near highways, railroads, and power lines. Normally, farm at least 30 feet from the road and ensure sure you do not farm in an environmentally sensitive area (such as a muddy river flood bank). And with herbicides, hay fields can be added.

The foundations are often troublesome in older buildings, and they are usually sprayed for pest protection or weeds. Consider visiting a nearby organic urban farm or community garden if you reside in an environment where you can find several tasty vegetables, along with gardeners who are eager to share the harvest.

Chapter 2: - Native American Herbs

Medicinal native plants have been cultivated from the forest and have been introduced for decades to home gardens. The production and usage of such medicinal plants in modern times reflect a safer form of life for the homesteader community and a safe re-supply strategy for the preppers and bug-out enthusiasts. Although these home remedies are never meant to take the place of qualified medical treatment, it's good to know that you're not powerless if you wind up by yourself. Below is a collection of 14 fantastic plants you'll find in the wild. Others can also be picked up at garden centers and attached to your private garden for medication.

Parsley [Petroselinum Crispum]

Parsley is a bitter, mild herb, which may boost your food flavor. Some find parsley to be just a curly green food garnish, but it lets foods like stews produce a more natural taste. Parsley can help indigestion as an added benefit. Parsley is grown chiefly annually, but it will stay evergreen all winter long in milder climates. Peregrine plants must mature to be large and bushy.

Mint types are numerous. Perhaps apply some mint to your iced tea for the season. Salt can freshen the air and help relax the stomach. But if you cultivate mint, note it's known as an unwanted herb. Mint spills over the Greenhouse and takes over. This is correctly contained in barrels.

Dill [Anethum graveolens]

Dill is an excellent flavoring for fish. It also assists in appetite, prevents poor breath, and has the additional benefits of minimizing swelling and cramps. It's easy to grow dill. It will draw helpful insects like wasps and other aggressive insects to your yard, too. It also saves a trip to Santa Barbara Dentist!

Thyme is a delicate herb in appearance. It is also used for potato, bean, and vegetable flavoring dishes. Thyme is widely found in cuisines like the Oriental, Italian and Provençal countries. Combine it with potatoes, poultry, and lamb. Soups and stews are also flavored with thyme. Thyme is a member of the family of mint. The most popular form is garden thyme with grey-green leaves and a minty, somewhat lemony scent.

Fennel is highly flavorful and spicy and is a primary component of absinthe along with Anise. Fennel is found in the Mediterranean region and grows well in dry areas near the coast or on the canal banks. The fennel's strongly aromatized leaves are similar in shape to dill. The bulb may be grilled or sautéed or eaten raw. Fennel bulbs are used for garnishing or occasionally added to salads.

The main component of 'Fines Herbes' is the new tarragon, the aristocrat of fresh herbs. A must-have for every Greenhouse with culinary herbs! It will transform an ordinary dish with its spicy anise flavor into a work of art. A little tarragon in a chicken salad creates a vast difference. The sauces, soups, and meat dishes are lovely. Try on vegetables. Any hearty dish is the alternative.

What's more enjoyable than seeing the family cat go somewhat berserk at the catnip smell? Yet catnip is more than merely a stimulant to felines. It may be used both as a relaxant and a diuretic and laxative. When you buy catnip outside, mind your cats love to crawl in and chew on it. Yet having catnips in your backyard can be a disincentive to rodents too.

Chives [Allium Schoenoprasum]

Chives belong to the family of garlic, which can be the best compliment to sour cream. Chives are often used for flavoring and are known to be French cuisine's "great herbs." Chives emerged in Asia but were used for about 5,000 years as an ingredient to add to milk. Eggs, fish, potatoes, salads, shellfish, and soups work well with chives. Chives are a healthy source of both beta-carotene and vitamin C.

St. John's wort is thought to alleviate depression and anxiety symptoms but should not be considered a cure. It can help relieve muscle discomfort, too. The rose was called this as the flowers grow about 24 June, John the Baptist's birthday. St. John's wort is also known as the weed; rosin rose, goat weed, chase-devil, or Klamath weed of Tipton. It is a standard ground cover in gardens, as it is resistant to drought. This is a well-known herbal remedy for depression but not used in cooking.

The fragrance of the noble leaves of the bay reminds you of balsam, clove, mint, and some even say, honey! It is best known for its use in heart-rending stews and other long-simmering dishes with a very salty, peppery, almost bitter flavor. Winter Savory [Satureja montana]

Winter Savory, a deliciously sweet culinary spice, brings an enticing taste to several dishes. Its antibacterial and anti-fungal properties are also used medicinally. Winter Savory, like its summer equivalent, is an aromatic Mint family culinary herb that supplements the strong flavor of seafood, beans, and poultry. While it loses some of this strength during the cooking process, Winter Savory retains aromatic qualities and is also used to spice liqueurs, creating a beautiful garnish to any salad.

Peppermint [Mentha piperita]

Like other mints, peppermint is famous for digestive help and air freshening. Yet peppermint is also a healthy source of magnesium, potassium, and vitamin B. Peppermint is a combination of mint and is a mix between water mint and spearmint. Peppermint oil may be used to spice but is effective as a natural pesticide as well. The symptoms of irritable bowel syndrome have been reported to decrease. Peppermint enjoys expansive soil and part shade. It spreads easily like other mints, so try planting it in containers.

Stevia is an enticing plant in nature and a natural sweetener. The added benefit is that calories don't exist. Stevia is part of the sunflower family, which is native to Western hemisphere subtropical and tropical areas. Though it is a perennial plant, it can only thrive in North America's milder climates. You can add stevia to your summer garden, anyway. Often known as Sweetleaf or sugar leaf, it is grown for its sweet berries. Stevia could be used as a sweetener and as a replacement for sugar.

Lemongrass stalks can include antioxidants such as beta-carotene and protection against inflammation of cancer and eyes. Lemongrass has a good citrus flavor. You should brew it in tea, then use it as a spice for herbs. You need to stay in at least Zone 9 to expand the outdoors. Outside it will grow up to six feet high, but if you grow it indoors, it would be significantly smaller.

Bee Balm is gaining popularity as a culinary plant, making a perfect addition to pizzas, salads, bread, and other recipes that complement the unique taste of the plant. Bergamot is minty yet mildly sweet, rendering Oregano a perfect alternative. Bergamot has a long tradition of being used by many Native Americans as a healing herb, including the Blackfeet. To treat minor injuries and bruises, the Blackfeet Indians used this hardy herb in poultices. A tea manufactured from the plant has also been used to treat infections of the mouth and throat triggered by gingivitis. The plant produces large amounts of a naturally occurring antiseptic, thymol, used in many brand names mouthwashes.

Oregano [Origanum vulgare]

Oregano also belongs to the mint family and is native to Eurasia and the Mediterranean warm climates. Oregano is a seasonal herb that may be cultivated annually in colder climates. This is often referred to as wild marjoram and is loosely related to honey marjoram. Oregano is a favorite herb in Italian American food and is used for flavoring. It gained attention in the United States during World War II as troops came home with a taste for the "pizza herb."

Cooked, mashed comfrey roots used as a topical remedy are good for inflammation, fractures, burns, and sprains. Only don't eat it: a new study suggests that eating in abundance is toxic to the liver. Root formulations are dangerous for internal usage owing to differences in the pyrrolizidine alkaloid content because they are considered pyrrolizidine-free. While historically used comfrey root tea, the danger of its pyrrolizidine alkaloids is substantial. Therefore, arrangements for comfrey root and young leaf need not be made in-house.

Burdock [Arctium]

The roots and leaves form an outstanding tonic for the liver and help purify the body and blood. Most people use burdock root to help them get rid of acne symptoms, which has an excellent impact on various skin issues, such as eczema. Render the dried root tincture in alcohol and drink 10-20 drops of tincture a day. Upon boiling water and discarding the water to eliminate bitterness, you may also consume the fresh leaves and roots.

Place one teaspoon of the dried root in one cup of hot water as a general liver/gallbladder tonic and promote digestion. A root-made tincture can be used three times a day. Some experts suggest tincture dependent on alcohol since the bitter values of alcohol are more soluble. One or two teaspoons of dried leaves may be applied as a moderate diuretic or appetite stimulant to one cup of boiling water and consumed as a decoction, up to three times a day.

Willow [Salix babylonica]

Use one which you can quickly recognize to prepare willow as a medicine. Weeping willow grows in all of North America. Though not local, it thrives in any moist environment, and its limp twigs and branches can be recognized. Over millennia the leaves and the bark were used as medicine. To produce an astringent, boil a palm with green leaves in one cup of water for 10 minutes. If no other medicinal care is appropriate, soak a clean cloth in this brew and apply it directly to burns, abscesses, carbuncles, and ulcers. Boil the bark scrapings off many twigs and boil them for 10 minutes in one cup of hot water for a gritty anti-diarrhea cocktail. Take a couple of sips every 2 hours, then start until the effects go down.

The bark of many other willow family types, including the black willow, has been in use since 400 B.C. for inflammation and pain management. Black willow bark, a precursor of aspirin, produces salicin. It was once customary for people to chew the pain and fever relief directly on the rasped bark.

Elderberry [Sambucas]

The elderberry is helpful when added to the skin while treating wounds. Elderflower is used orally in many nations, including Germany, to combat respiratory illnesses such as colds and flu. Some evidence suggests that chemicals in elderflowers and elderberries may help reduce inflammation of mucous membranes, such as the sinuses, and help alleviate nasal congestion. Elder may have propensities to be anti-inflammatory, antiviral, and anticancer. Dosage is simple. Eat jam or wine made from elderberries only. But be mindful that the raw berries are slightly poisonous. They could have medication reactions with diuretics (water pills), diabetic medications, antibiotics, laxatives, theophylline (Theodor), or immunosuppressant medicines.

Black Walnut [Juglans nigra]

The walnut green husks have many applications in traditional medicine. One teaspoon of the dried green husk content in one cup of hot water can create a terrible degustation, the agent that expels tea. Sip for a day in one cup, and repeat for seven days. New walnut husks on minor cuts and wounds (they also stain the skin like iodine) were used to replace iodine tincture as an antiseptic.

Jewelweed [Impatiens capensis]

When you come into touch with poison ivy, oak, or sumac, find some jewelweed (Impatiens capensis), smash the moist, purplish plant into a slimy paste, and wash it all over the skin involved. Wash the jewelweed mush away with clean water after 2 minutes of touching. You will get minimal or no poison ivy response when you can manage so within 30 to 45 minutes of exposure to ivy. While discovering the Jewelweed took more time, you will always feel some relaxation by using it as a shower. Jewelweed is going to cool poison ivy's itch.

Milk Thistle [Silybum marianum]

This herb is another excellent item to pack in your medicine chest. With its ability to reduce inflammation, this herb has been known to have some rather impressive results. Milk thistle serves to boost liver function and, in some instances, has even been seen to reverse the effects of cirrhosis. If you have any inflammation whatsoever, simply apply some Milk Thistle directly to the area afflicted, and you will see results.

Red Clover [Trifolium pretense]

Red Clover is a powerful herbal antibiotic that can significantly boost the immune system. This herb has even been known to increase the red blood cell count in those that use it. Interestingly enough, Red Clover is also a natural anticoagulant and can loosen up blood clots in a relatively rapid fashion. This, in turn, provides a general boost in health no matter what you may be facing.

Yarrow [Achillea millefolium]

This herb can get to work on inflammation and congestion in the human body almost immediately. This herbal antibiotic also works well against injuries. As soon as it is applied to an injured site, it gets to work cleansing the wound and promoting the formation of blood platelets for quick and effective healing.

This herb is an excellent antibiotic fighter, and its best work is done to reduce inflammation and boost the immune system. Just apply a small amount of this herbal antibiotic to the skin, and you will be able to enhance your body's ability to stand up to and survive all manner of airborne illnesses. Give this herbal Gauche Antibiotic a try!

Anise [Pimpinella anisum]

This herb works out just great as an herbal antibiotic, killing most bacteria right on the spot. This herbal antibiotic also works on the urinary system, helping to clear up any incontinence that someone may face and putting the whole body into a kind of detox, almost immediately. So drink up folks, because this Herbal Anise is on me!

Chervil [Anthriscus cerefolium]

Chervil has a real proven ability to kill bacteria, get rid of headaches, and calm upset stomachs. It is the latter from which many a camper has benefited. It is common practice for many survivalists to simply pop a chervil leaf in their mouth and chew to relieve their upset stomach. I have tried this myself and can say that it does wonders.

Cloves [Syzygium aromaticum]

In a similar fashion to chervil, cloves have been placed directly into many dental patients' mouths to kill bacteria and curb inflammatory agents. This herb also works as a mild form of pain reliever and can numb up a bad toothache if needed successfully.

Sage [Salvia apiana]

This medicinal herb takes survival medicine to a whole new life to successfully reduce all manner of pain and kill bacterial infections on the spot. If you have fallen and sustained an injury, just a minimal application of this healing herb will work to alleviate any pain that you may feel. Another great benefit of herbal sage is its ability to treat asthma.

Valerian [Valeriana officinalis]

Valerian is also another trendy nighttime home remedy to deal with your anxiety. It contains some elements of mild tranquilizing properties that will almost guarantee you and will get you a good night's sleep; however, without all dreaded and the weird hangover feeling early in the morning that you may sometimes have to get with some other pharmaceuticals.

Lemon Balm [Melissa officinalis]

Lemon Balm also is known as 'Melissa Officinalis which is one herbal supplement and tea to

Some studies suggested that the use of lemon balm can decrease insomnia, anxiety, hyperexcitation, and fatigue.

A lemon balm extract should be taken 300mg at breakfast and 300mg at dinner, which may help reduce insomnia mainly due to a decrease in nervousness and decreased agitation, guilt, hyperexcitation, and fatigue too.

Eschscholtzia californica, which is a tension-relieving, anti-anxiety, sedative, and antispasmodic herb. California poppy also helps with sleeplessness and quells a headache as well as muscular spasm from stress. Some gentle and non-addictive actions are much safer for children and the elderly.

Wild Lettuce [Lactuca virosa]

Wild Lettuce is the species of lactic vireos, a mild tranquilizer that may be used to calm a nervous or overactive nervous system. It is very suitable for anxious children or even adolescents. It majorly helps with insomnia. It is also a general pain reliever and antispasmodic that can primarily be used for short coughs.

Rosemary [Salvia Rosmarinus]

The herb that makes chicken sing and soups taste excellent help treat headaches, nervous tension, a nervous stomach, cleanse the face, and can even help to stimulate hair growth. Great in teas, oils, and soaks.

White Willow Bark [Salicin]

Salicin is an active ingredient in willow barks, and this ingredient is converted into salicylic acid in your body. This bark can reduce the level of prostaglandins that is a hormone-like compound in your body. This compound can increase inflammation, pain, and aches in your body. White willow bark is entirely safe for your stomach. This bark can be used to get relief from muscle pains and menstrual cramps, arthritis, muscle pain, and knee pain. It is also good to reduce swelling.

Valerian Root [Valeriana officinalis]

Valerian is an herb, and its roots are used to make medicine for sleep disorders. It is a common herb used with the combination of hops and lemon balms. The valerian root can cause drowsiness and is ideal for those who have insomnia. If you are using sleeping pills, then you are advised to treat it with valerian root. The women are suffering from menstrual cramps and symptoms of menopause; they can use this herb for their treatment. The extracts and oil of the valerian root are used to flavor different food items and beverages.

Arnica [Arnica montana]

It is an excellent herbal rub that can be used to cure your pain, acute injuries, and pain after surgery, injury, and extreme sports. This herb is helpful for its anti-inflammatory properties.

Ginseng [Panax ginseng]

There are various varieties of this herb, and Panax ginseng is the most common variety. It is known as Korean ginseng. Ginsenosides have anticancer and anti-inflammatory properties.

Turmeric [Curcuma longa]

Turmeric contains curcumin that has distinguished antioxidant properties. It has anti-inflammatory, stomach-soothing, and antibacterial benefits. It is good to reduce tenderness by stimulating adrenal glands to amplify the hormone that reduces inflammation. Turmeric is good for the protection of the liver and helps you to solve digestive problems.

There are many benefits to the use of aloe Vera, such as it is helpful to treat constipation and skin disorders. It can fight tumors and colorectal cancers. Aloe vera is available in the form of supplements and gel.

The aloe vera is famous for its healing properties, and it is specifically used to treat sunburn and relieve pain. The key symptoms of arthritis are inflammation and painful joints; you can take the help of aloe vera to treat rheumatoid arthritis.

Calendula [Calendula officinalis]

This plant is famous for its antimicrobial and anti-inflammatory properties. It is suitable for topical use to heat abrasions, treat infections and infected mucous membranes. It is easy to buy calendula herbal medicines from food stores and apply your wounds. If you want to treat internal disorders, you can make a calendula tea with warm water (1 cup) and one tablespoon.

Chamomile was a traditional medicine used thousands of years ago for the treatment of anxiety and upset stomach. The herb is used with a combination of other plants to get lots of health benefits. If you are suffering from heartburn, upset stomach, nausea, and sickness, you can use chamomile. It also proves helpful for sore mouth and cancer. If you have any skin irritation, chamomile can help you to heal your wounds.

This root is similar to white cylinders and famous for its sweet taste. This herb is found in the candy section of the grocery store. This plant has excellent properties to heal wounds wreaked on your body. This herb is perfect for extracting bacteria and toxins from your injury. It can heal bruises and burns. You can create a poultice with a marshmallow and apply it to your wounds for speed healing.

Passionflower [Passiflora incarnata]

The top part of the passion flower plant is used to make medicine for the sleep problems, anxiety, gastrointestinal ailments, nervousness, and withdrawal symptoms of the narcotic drugs. It is equally beneficial for asthma, hysteria, seizures, nervousness, irregular heartbeat, and high blood pressure. It can also be used to treat skin burns, pains, and swelling.

Its extracts are used in the food and beverages to flavor them. It can be used with a combination of other drugs to prop up tranquility and relaxation. You can combine it with the hops, skullcap, kava, valerian, and German chamomile. The chemicals found in the passionflower can make you calm and promote good sleep by relieving the effects of muscle spasms.

One study has found it has to be as effective as benzodiazepine drugs, but the only difference is without drowsiness. Passionflower may also help you to feel an emotionally balanced and exceptionally beneficial way.

Nonetheless, suppose you suffer from exaggerated emotions. In that case, this is by far one of the most efficient home remedies to deal with anxiety, and it needs to be part of your daily regimen.

Conclusion

The Native American belief in the interconnectedness of human beings and nature is difficult to explain. As ancestors, all part of one large and at least theoretically prosperous family, they looked at all living things and some physical facets of nature, such as rivers, mountains, and climates.

The Native Americans claimed that a poor interaction with some facets of nature also induced illness. While there were clear explanations for certain forms of injury, such as snake bites and burns, it was challenging to describe internal diseases. The Native Americans thought that the angry spirits of animals, who took vengeance for insults they got in childhood, were more likely to cause "invisible" diseases. "An animal ghost will cause problems if reference is not given to the body after it has been murdered," according to historian William Corlett. Since Native Americans assumed that humans and nature were closely connected, nearly any thought or behavior might have adverse effects if it displayed contempt for nature. For instance, spitting on fire could rage the spirits and result in disease.

Nature, of course, has not always been regarded with apprehension. Much as when they were angry, the spirits of animals and other facets of personality could be dangerous; they might also be beneficial when they were happy. For one, the Native Americans believed that herbs and even animals' organs were full of enormous healing powers. During their various curing rituals, they also called on the spirits of animals for help. It was believed that multiple species had unique characteristics and qualities, such as cunning, intellect, and courage. Native Americans may call for individual animal spirits during healing rituals, asking each in return to share their unique gifts with the person being healed. Still, of course, doctors are unlikely to consider calling on the spirits of eagles and bears to regulate blood pressure or cure arthritis. Depending on how it is handled, they are very mindful of nature's ability to cure or hurt. For example, prolonged exposure to sunlight can cause cancer. Still, when the sun is used correctly (approximately 15 minutes of everyday exposure), it makes the body produce vitamin D necessary for healthy bones. Nutrients are filled with the foods we consume, such as vitamin A, iron, folate, and sodium are essential to life in the correct quantity; in abundance, all of them can be dangerous. Since the keys to wellbeing are peace and order, who does not benefit from learning a lesson from the Native American people? The way to start is by treating with the highest regard the world around us.

BOOK 2

Native American Herbal Dispensatory

Introduction

Native American medicine relates to over 500 nations' combined clinical practices. Native medicine is almost forty thousand years old. The particular activities differed between tribes, but everything is based on the universal idea that man is an integral part of nature and that a matter of balance is health. When interrelationships are valued, nurtured, and sustained in harmony, the natural world then moves as a consequence. The natural world cannot be seen by the mind and does not engage in science directly and intuitively. Much like a human being's inner life cannot be determined, nature has persuasive forces that need to be incorporated for balance. Just now has reporting started and has been limited to findings, so it is incomplete. Native medicine values all life and is not just a body of science or methodology that is scholarly. For fear of exploitation, Native American elders typically do not disclose their knowledge.

The balance between inner life and available actions is tackled in Native American medicine. They all consider the body, mind, soul, thoughts, social circle, and lifestyle. The choice and desires of a patient are often respected to establish harmony. Bodywork, naturopathy, bone setting, midwifery, hydrotherapy, botanical, and nutritional medicine can be included in every Native American healer's strategy. Often used are ceremonial and ritual medicines. Many of this has been forgotten as only by living practitioners has this undocumented living practice survived. More Native Americans have been involved in protecting their culture, and Native American medicine today is as fluid as ever with this effort.

Chapter 1: Native American Medicine

Through a robust oral tradition, Native Americans' generations have obtained medical information over the past 40,000 years. The interconnection between humanity, ecology, and the spiritual realm is emphasized by indigenous medical philosophy. A person of medicine studies the relationships of the patient with other individuals, the individual's physical well-being and establishes a holistic approach for healing. A combination of therapies and experiences are used to treat and cure the patient. These may include herbs, ceremony, music, prayer and sweating.

To cure cardiovascular disorders and many other cancers and diseases, black cohosh, a traditional medicinal herb, was used. The effectiveness of Native American medical therapies is now accepted by western medicine. Conventional and new medicines are not inherently mutually exclusive. Thus, they can be used in concert with each other. Any of the plants used by Native American physicians can now be found in retail stores around the country. They include black cohosh that is used to treat cardiovascular issues. Similarly, Echinacea is used to cure infections.

Treatment approach

Native American medicine is a complete framework that balances every sphere of one's life, including lifestyle and social interactions with one inner world. Native medicine assumes that in the divine realm, the roots of every imbalance lie. In the course of every recovery procedure, spiritual approaches are vital. Including fees and rates, clinical guidelines are often clearly and uniquely tailored for the patient. They require, as part of the healing method, the process of fee negotiation. The Healing Elder seems to have the most healing strength, and the elder practitioner loses his prestige as a powerful healer when treatment fails. The person in need of healing makes a proposition to the doctor of medicine and waits to see if it is approved. Face-to-face, they rarely negotiate. The customer leaves the bid outside the healer's door, and if it remains there till the morning, it means that it has not been approved, and one can go somewhere. Once they understand, therapy will, for example, start with a behavioral prescription, a pledge, a selfless act, genuine repentance, or scaling a holy mountain. Techniques include self-inquiry and discovery to ascertain whether there is a need for a dietary improvement, prayer, herbs, massage, a sweat lodge ritual or a vision quest.

The main objective is to alter the patient's comprehension of the world through a healthier self-concept, increased acceptance of others and behavior adjustments. The healer's goal is to treat sickness and change the patient's overall approach towards life and the world around him. Native American medicine combines science as well as spirit with the onset of new technology. They mostly use herbal interventions and pharmaceuticals. We can explain this by narrating a Native American story on the use of herbal medicine. Barb, a wife, mother and lawyer, is still fighting breast cancer. She did what she could normally do, and cancer continued to spread despite all her efforts. She met with an Indian elder named Big Nose in a sweat lodge. He wanted to understand what she was doing or what hadn't changed in her life. Deep inside, as a mother-wife and lawyer, she thought she was a loser, and now she's healing herself. It was the pessimistic self-talk that needed to end, Big Nose told her. Barb decided to let go of her arrogant thought that she would be cured and enjoy the moment with her family due to this relationship. There is another story that talks of a woman who had had extreme arthritis. She was desperately looking for the right healer. To facilitate recovery, medicine men go further and beyond the current problem and understand radical improvement is often required. The shifts are primary, and herbs are secondary, along with massage and prayer. Right relationships, the correction of relationships with oneself, families, members of the society and the spiritual environment are all effects of disruption of relationships and disease development.

Training

Native American healers, through apprenticeships, educate their students. For preparation, several weeks of testing the purpose and dedication of a student are vital. An apprentice gains patience and respect and acquires knowledge. Native medicine is still an oral tradition. It cannot be taught in an academic setting. Students may learn the skills required only by experience, and only when the patient is ready does the older instructor encourage them to begin a medical practice.

The Main Role of Ceremonies

A crucial aspect of traditional aboriginal healing is the ritual. Due to the close relationship between physical & spiritual well-being, body and soul should heal together. Popular healing rituals encourage well-being by representing traditional concepts of the world, creator, and spirit. Prayer, drumming, chants, poems, legends & the use of several religious artifacts may be part of them. Wherever an ill person requires healing, healers can perform ceremonies, but the traditions are sometimes performed in sacred places. The unique buildings are also mentioned as the Medicine Lodges for recovery. Traditional healing rituals are considered holy wherever they take place & are only performed by the native healers & local spiritual facilitators. The Non-Natives can take part only by invitation. Native powwows, on the other hand, have grown today into most social and cultural activities that include indigenous music, singing, drumming, regalia, and food. Most powwows welcome all persons.

The Medicine Wheel and the Four Directions

Medicine Wheel, also referred to as the Holy Hoop, has been used for health and healing by thousands of diverse Native American tribes. Also, Father Heaven, Spirit Tree, and Mother Earth represent the Four Paths, symbolizing the dimensions of well-being and life cycles. There are several different shapes that Medicine Wheel could take. It could be artwork, or a real structure on the ground, such as an artifact or painting. Over the past few decades, hundreds of thousands, even, of the medicine wheels that have been constructed on tribal lands in North America. Movement is circular in Medicine Wheel & in the Native American formalities, & typically in the direction of the clock, or the direction is sun-wise. It tends to sync with nature's powers, like gravity & sun's rising & setting.

Meanings of the Four Directions

Medicine Wheel is viewed differently by various tribes. Usually, each of the Four Directions (West, East, North, and South) is represented by a distinctive hue, such as red, black, yellow, & white, representing human races for some. The Directions may also indicate:

- **Stages of life:** the birth, youth, adulthood (or elder), and death
- **Element of nature:** sun (or fire), water, earth, and air
- **Animals:** Bear, Eagle, Buffalo, Wolf, & many more
- **Seasons of the year:** spring, summer, winter, fall
- **Aspects of life:** spiritual, emotional, intellectual, physical
- **Ceremonial plants:** sweet grass, tobacco,cedar, sage

For a broad range of medical uses, Alaska Native, Native American & healers of Native Hawaiian all have a long tradition of using the native or indigenous plants. Medicinal plants are as varied as tribes that use them and their uses. Beyond their medical effects, before Western settlement, native plants were the staple of aboriginal people's diet. Today, the indigenous plant is central to current generations' attempts to enhance nutritional wellbeing. "Waianae Diet" & "Pre-Captain Diet Cook" are trying to decrease fat, empty calories, & additives. At the same time, they are trying to facilitate a healthier balanced diet by restoring indigenous foods' role.

Intersections of Traditional and Western Healing

Today, the issue of either depending on conventional native healing practices or pursuing Western medical care is frequently confronted by Native Americans of both groups. The two cultures existed in tandem relatively until recently, with really no intersections between them. However, now, the continuum of health services can be accessed by Native Americans. Within tribal communities, most traditional healers are still practicing independently. To organize treatment for Native American patients, other healers can collaborate with Western-trained foremost care physicians. Some healthcare facilities, often at the exact location, provide both conventional and Western medicine. In certain areas, rather than by tribal health centers or hospitals, patients of Native Americans receive traditional healing from inside the local tribal population. In the Upper Plains Tribes of Lakota and Dakota, & Mandan, Hidatsa, & Arikara, (MHA), tribal members arrange for the services by directly calling nearby healers. Many Western-trained doctors often recommend patients to conventional healers and may sometimes assist a specific patient in coordinating traditional and Western medicine.

Chapter 2: Herbal Medicine

Herbal medicine is an ancient art that has been utilized for centuries, and many see it as one of the last forms of natural healing. It's safe to say you are surrounded by herbs, a broad term for plant material found in a range of varieties. Most people have considered these plants "medicinals." But what exactly does this term mean, and what makes it unique from other types of medicine?

The word "medicinal" comes to us via the Latin phrase meaning "to heal." This reflects how these plants have been used for centuries to prevent or treat disease. Indeed, herbs are one of our oldest medicines. Early on many of them were the only form of medicine known.

The word "medicinals" has come to refer to plants with healing properties that have been used in traditional herbal medicines for centuries, as well as other substances such as minerals and animal parts. Herbs are typically highly diluted or made into extracts by various methods, including cold-pressing, boiling the whole plant material in water, percolating liquid through dry plant material; herb teas can be steeped from any number of herbs (e.g., ginger tea). This is not true all the time, but this substance will often require some sort of heat processing that removes/destroys some beneficial compounds within it.

Buying Herbal Medicine

If you walk down any city street, you'll probably be able to find an herbalist shop. This might be in culturally specific areas of a city or areas with other medical stores nearby. They may be near stores that focus on New Age or equivalent practices. Wherever you find them, you should go through the stores and check the products before purchasing anything.

If you are purchasing your herbs in loose form (i.e., where you can tell that it's a twig or berry or flower), then there are some things you want to look for.

- The herbs should look like what they represent. Even dried, there shouldn't be a massive difference in color or texture. Whites will tend to change to cream colors as the petals dry, and reds/blues will get darker. But if you're expecting an orange flower and you receive a purple one or white one instead, it's probably not the right plant.
- Following up on that, make sure the colors are bright. They shouldn't be dull or brown.
- Herbs should smell like what they're supposed to. If you have an aromatic herb, you should be able to smell it, even in a dried form. If it smells like nothing or like grass, then it might not match.
- While checking over the herbs, make sure everything in the container looks the same. If there are pieces that don't look like they belong, then they probably don't.
- The herbs should be stored in the correct containers. They should be in dark glass jars or other containers where they won't be exposed to light and air easily.
- Make sure that any herbal supplements you purchase have the proper labeling. Consider the labels on prescriptions: they tend to include things like the scientific name of the product, daily dosage, the weight of each pill, warnings, and any additives. So, you want to look for the same on your herbal supplement bottles.

When looking for a reputable local source, ask local herbalists or doctors for recommendations. You can also look at the websites for different herbal practitioner organizations to see if they have any suggestions.
You want to follow some of the key steps as those above once you receive your purchase for online purchasing. Choose to buy things from reputable online shops.

Growing Herbs

You can grow your herbs from seeds, cuttings of existing plants, root division, or simply purchase the plant from a reputable nursery. Some herbs need a lot of space to grow, while others do well in pots. Herbs are divided by where they can grow, either in a kitchen garden, flower garden, or larger areas. Most herbs you'll succeed at home need about eight hours of sunlight daily and well-draining soil. You can find out how to grow your particular herbs of choice by checking their growing requirements online.
Once you have your plant, you'll need to make sure it thrives. Follow its requirements. For example, rosemary, one of my favorite kitchen garden herbs, does well in my gardening zone and loves full sun. It's placed on my back porch in a pot and gets as much sun as it needs. I water it once a week in spring and fall, but more often in the summer. However, the calendula plants in my flower garden hate the summer in my area. So, I grow them, so they bloom in spring and fall instead of the summer. Because I know a lot about my garden zone and I know the requirements for rosemary and calendula, I can make sure the plants are thriving.

You'll also need to choose the best time of year to harvest from your plant. Leaves can be harvested right after they open, though be sure not to remove more than ¼–⅓ of the plant's total leaves since they need them for their survival. The leaves are harvested in the spring or summer, usually during a sunny day. Flowers can be harvested once they are in full bloom, usually during the first day of the bloom. Many flowers bloom in summer, so you'll harvest them then. The fall is the time for roots. Most plants whose roots will be harvested need to be alive for years (yes, years!) before they're harvested. So, if you want to harvest your dandelion roots, you'll need to leave them on your lawn for four years, give or take.

Once you've harvested from your plants, you'll need to determine how to store them. If you're going to use them quickly, use them on the same day you harvest them. You can also store them in the freezer. But my preferred method for storing my kitchen garden herbs is to dry them. Find a dry, dark area in your house and dry your flowers and leaves there. Once all the moisture is gone from the plant (they should feel room temperature, not cool or damp), store them in dark glass containers away from sunlight. And there you have it! Your first harvested herbs. They'll last dried for about a year and in the freezer for about six months. Otherwise, use them immediately after harvesting.

Preparation

Personal Herbal Medicines

Personal herbal medicine would be an herbal medicine, most probably a combination, that you could a hundred percent rely on for getting better whenever you got a fever again. With time you would feel so confident in that remedy that you would also recommend it to other people, people that you care about. This herbal medicine is not necessarily supposed to be one that you make. Instead, it can be a remedy (a premade one) that you have always felt that it worked every time you used it.

Can You Make Herbal Medicines by Yourself?

If you haven't guessed it already, yes, you can! And the day you do so, it will change your life. How so? First of all, you will need a purpose to be making an herbal medicine, to use it as a cure. When you go through all the complicated stuff, which can be explained as the mixing process, you will have a result. This result may end up disappointing you in the end, but that will only mean that you have to try again to find a newer and better medicine.

Let's consider that you have the final result, and you need to use it. After successfully using a medicine that you made yourself, the feeling that you would feel right away will be priceless.

The next thing you will know is that you will be trying to make newer medicines due to the confidence in your last success, and you will find yourself constantly recommending your remedy to the people you think need it.

Where to Get All the Herbs?

Most of the herbs can all be grown in your kitchen garden very quickly. It finally comes to the point that you have to be committed to this completely. You will find yourself willing enough to plant little amounts of all of these herbs in small pots if you are. You will also have to take responsibility for these herbs, so you will have to water them and take care of their fertilizers. Soon enough, this responsibility will turn into love for those plants.

If, in any case, you don't find it easy to go through all the processes to produce herbal ingredients yourself, you can always go to the local superstore. There, you will find all the herbs you were looking for and some that you have never even heard about.

Tools Needed to Make Herbal Medicines

In the old times, the people who were supposed to sell medicines and spices (basically all things related to herbs) to people were called apothecaries. These guys started wearing masks with pointy beaks and were called doctors in their times because that was what they mostly did for a living; sell medicines. Apothecaries were also supposed to make them merchandise themselves. Although they are the professional ancestors of pharmacists, for whom the machinery has been changed for the good, the basic preparation tools were the same for both of them, and so will they be for you. You would mostly need the following things to make herbal medicines of your own:

- Saucepans of various sizes.
- Wooden spoons and spatulas.
- Jars, tins, pots, and other containers.
- Mortar and pestle.
- Knives.
- Scissors.
- Tweezers.
- Strainers.

In this part, we will talk about something similar; how do domestic herbalists or, simply, people at home, are supposed to make medicines' doses for different types of herbs. The herb can be a bark (cinnamon), a bud (cardamom), powder (turmeric), a leaf (basil or mint), and etcetera. You may not notice this at first, but you will realize that every resultant form of medicine cannot be achieved from all of the herbs when I start the list. The list is as follows:

- **Food medicines:** The simplest and the easiest way to eat herbal medicines are to involve them in dishes or simply, your regular everyday food. So if someone was supposed to take high amounts of mint, to wake up for more time or to clean his digestive system (because that is the.benefit of mint), he can go straight up to get a mint margarita and down it as soon as possible.

- **Decoctions:** This is what you would call the way to take medicines for some things that are not chewable, such as bark or a stem. What an herbalist does is that he breaks the herb into many small pieces, so it is almost as small as table salt, and then boils them in water. You keep on boiling them until the water level is decreased to a half or a third. This process is doing because it is extracting all the nutritional value of the herb into the water. The water is then taken as a dose.

- **Powders:** If the herbs can help, we dried them up and then ground them into refined grains, and then the medicine's dose can also be in the form of its powder. This is often the case where you combine two herbs, and their combination has both the parent characteristics. Interesting fact; besides eating an herb fresh from the leaf, this is the purest dose that one can get if it is suitable for the body.

- **Syrups:** Syrup is the type of dosage that is often used to disguise unpleasant herbs. First, for syrups to be made, the herb is supposed to be converted into such a form that it can be dissolved into an addable liquid. Both of them are then mixed, and you have a resultant that tastes disgusting. That is where the sweetener comes into action. It is used to make the syrup close to something that can be considered eaten, especially by kids.

- **Aromatic Waters:** Sorry if I fooled you there. Aromatic waters are not necessarily supposed to be water, which is drinkable. These liquids are often low boiling point liquids that are supposed to produce various smells when given even the smallest heats. Their dosage types are fumes that are supposed to one of the two things about to be explained:

1. Inhaled for their unique smell.
2. Inhaled for treatment of the respiratory system.

- **Ointments:** Ointments or balms are supposed to be herbal remedies' dosages that are mostly applied to wounds, whether it is external or internal. They are known to work the best when applied to strained muscles. They can also be applied to recovering sprained joints.

Chapter 3: Using Fresh Plants

With herbs, it's important to get the most out of them when you can. That means being selective about where and when you pick herbs, and using fresh herbs in your preparations when possible. Even just drying your herbs for use, later on, is a time-honored practice of herbalists everywhere, especially if you intend to use the herb regularly.

To many herbalists, the words fresh and dried are often used interchangeably. However, there is a difference between new and dried herbs.

Dried herbs have been dehydrated or extracted by one means or another. When the herbal medicine is made into a tea, it's also possible to use the herb if it has been made into a syrup, tincture, tea-based oil or salve.

Fresh herbs, on the other hand, haven't been processed in any way. This means that their natural powers are still present. Some of these herbs are more potent than those with which they have been processed, and some might also contain natural chemicals that give them a special effect if used correctly.

It's important to note as well that not all fresh herbs are edible. Many look quite nasty and might even cause you to harm if you eat them raw or improperly prepared. Therefore, it's important to know which herbs are edible and non-toxic before you start using them.

Harvesting

Harvesting herbs is a time-honored practice at best. But it's also a task that cultivators, farmers, and naturalists have been involved in for centuries. Some herbs are often collected from the wild, while others are grown on farms and hedgerows.

Herbal medicine is all about respecting the plants you use, whether they're wild or grown by hand. That means harvesting them when they're in their most potent form. For example, harvesting mint during its blooming period will yield a far more potent product than if you harvest it before or after this time.

Other herbs have to be harvested in a certain way or at a specific time. For example, many types of ginger are considered to be "hot," rather than "cold" as one might assume. Therefore, the root is harvested when it's dormant to avoid getting burned from it.

Herbs can be harvested as soon as they're ready for use. For example, harvesting mint leaves before they flower will guarantee that you have a good supply through the summer and well into the fall.

When harvesting fresh herbs, make sure to cut them off at their roots with a sharp blade or pruning shears. This will prevent them from drying out and losing the properties that give them their curative powers. However, if you can't harvest herbs while they're still fresh, you can store them in a glass jar with a tightly lidded lid in the refrigerator for up to 3 weeks.

As an herbalist or general practitioner, it's important to think about the conditions your patients live under and what sort of environments they're exposed to. This is one of the most essential parts of being an herbalist; learning about the plant life surrounding us and how we can use it to our advantage.

Drying

There are many reasons why one might dry herbs. One is to make an herbal medicine stronger and more potent, while another is to make it easier to store. But perhaps the most common reason one would dry herbs is so they can be stored for a long time without losing their potency.

Drying your herbs the right way will ensure that they remain fresh as well. Overdying them could ruin the whole batch and turn it into ashen, useless pieces of plant matter. Not to mention that it could damage the herbs you hope to use next.

Drying herbs will remove moisture but no other vital components such as essential oils and enzymes. To get the most out of your herbs, use a method that removes moisture but leaves all the rest of the goodness intact. The best way is to dry them slowly in an oven at low temperatures and low humidity.

To dry herbs using an oven, you'll need to sort them into sections and put each in a separate container. Then put them all in a single oven that is set to the lowest temperature that your oven can go and with the lowest humidity possible. For example, if you have a convection oven that reaches temperatures of 180 degrees Fahrenheit then set it for 180 degrees Fahrenheit.

Alternatively, you can use a dehydrator to dry herbs. Set the temperature to the lower end of what your dehydrator can manage, and make sure that you add moisture to the settings. This will ensure that your herbs don't get dried out completely. A good, slow drying process will be safe for your herbs and ensure they retain most of their nutrients.

How long does it take to dry herbs? This largely depends on how much moisture there is in them in the first place. Broccoli contains about 90% water for instance, while mint contains 96%.

Herbs that have more moisture in them will require a longer drying time. You need to allow plenty of time for every batch if you want them to dry all the way through. This will ensure that no mold forms and turn brown all over instead of just on the top, where black mold would form.

If your herbs are completely dried out, you can start thinking about adding them to recipes or turning them into tea leaves. If you're having trouble with this, you may want to bake them at a lower temperature.

If they're still a little wet, it can be helpful to place them on a paper towel and use another paper towel to press down on the top of them so they'll dry out more quickly.

Chapter 4: Extractions

Extracting is a wonderful thing. It's what allows us to very easily make things like tinctures, salves and oils from herbs. Through the extraction process, we get the healing phytochemicals our bodies crave and that make herbs useful medicine.

This list is by no means a comprehensive picture of all the things you can do with plants so please take it as an introduction to making medicinal preparations rather than a complete guide.

But what exactly is an extraction? An extraction is a technique where you put whole herbs into a liquid, and the plant's essential oils and phytochemicals are extracted from the plants. Extractions also involve drying out the herbs, so they retain their properties and are safe to use or add other ingredients to create new formulas.

Terms

There are a few useful terms to know about, especially if you want to use herbs as a healing agent. Some of the most important ones include:

Tonics: Tonics are usually taken in small doses and have acted in the body, but not necessarily direct action on disease. These can be used for overall conditioning or promotion of health.

Tonics do not have to be taken internally; they can be applied externally as well. For example, as an ointment for skin conditions or to promote general healing. Tonics can also be taken in the form of teas.

Tonic herbs are generally low in potency. Examples of tonics include marshmallow root, motherwort, and goldenseal root.

Herbal tea: An herbal tea is made by steeping dried herbs in hot water. Herbal teas can be made from fresh herbs, but dried is most common for medicinal preparation. Herbal teas are often mixed with other herbs such as peppermint, chamomile, and lemon balm.

Herbal teas can be used topically in the form of a poultice or bath to soothe aches and pains and promote health. They can be taken as a tisane or infused in a cup of hot water. Some herbal teas such as chamomile can be useful for children with upset stomachs or upset emotional states.

Decoction: Decoctions are made by simmering, or boiling whole herbs in water. This is a great way of using herbs with high potency.
Infusions: Infusions are made by steeping the herbal material in hot water. They are usually done in whole food, such as fruit, and even chocolate or honey. Herbal infusions can be taken as teas or tinctures.

Tinctures: Tinctures are made by steeping dried herbs in alcohol for up to 90 days or until dry. Tinctures are usually used to preserve the phytochemicals in the herb, although there are also tinctures that have been simply infused with alcohol that can be used. A tincture contains a much lower potency of herbal material than a tea or infusion.

Tea: Tea is made by steeping herbs in hot water. Herbal teas can be made from fresh herbs, too but dried is most common for use as a medicinal preparation. Herbal teas are often mixed with other herbs such as peppermint, chamomile, and lemon balm.

Herbal teas can be used topically in the form of a poultice or bath to soothe aches and pains and promote health. They can be taken as tea bags or infused in a cup of hot water. Some herbal teas such as chamomile can be helpful for children with upset stomachs or upset, emotional states.

Equipment

Equipment you may need for herbal smoking blends will include:

1. **Digital scale (continuous or digital)**
   This is useful if you want to get an exact measurement of what's going into your blend. Weigh out your herbs and ingredients carefully.

2. **lass or metal jars with tight-fitting lids**

You can use any glass jar; just make sure it's clean and doesn't have any scratches on the inside. Make sure that you label them well so you don't confuse one for another.

3. **Two plastic spoons**
   One spoon for stirring your ingredients and the other for scooping out the herbs. You can also use a metal spoon or even chopsticks.

4. **A sharp knife (such as an X-Acto Knife)**
   A sharp, small knife is great for chopping herbs that are particularly thick and hard to get through.

5. **A coffee grinder or blender (optional)**
   If you have a coffee grinder or blender, you can use this instead of chopping herbs by hand if you'd like. If you're using a coffee grinder, grind the spices into powder first. If you're using a blender, then don't grind them in the blender - you'll just end up with green sludge.

6. **A shredder**
   This is useful for getting through different items like chocolate or carrots to be used in tinctures.

7. **A double boiler**
   A double boiler is useful for preparing herbal teas and infusions, making extracts, or using tinctures.

8. **Distilled water (optional)**
   Distilled water is effective at cutting the sharp, spicy taste of some herbs like mint or ginger. Distilling your own water is much more cost-effective than buying it in a bottle from a store - but you'll need distilled water if it's needed for extraction with alcohol later on.

9. **Various containers**
   You can use a small jar, a pot for a double boiler, a glass bottle with a cap, or any other sort of container. Whatever works best for you!

10. **A healing stone (optional)**
    A healing stone is good for grounding and centering while you're doing your crafting. It's particularly useful when trying to stay calm or if you're getting stressed out. Just hold the stone in your hand while crafting and try to center yourself around it.

Basic Extracts

All of these extracts can be made with fresh herbs, dried herbs, or both. Some of them can be made with an alcohol base but most are safe for ingestion without it.

Extracting Herbs in Water

These extracts are made from herbs with high water content. For example, you can use fresh ginger and mint leaves for this but you can't use fresh parsley or other herbs with lower water content and won't infuse well in boiling water.

1. Chop the herb into manageable pieces.
2. Place the herbs into a container with boiling water, making sure to cover it completely.
3. Let it soak for 10 minutes at least; more if you'd like to make an even stronger extract (up to overnight is fine).
4. Strain the herbs out using a strainer, cheesecloth, or another method.
5. Let the liquid cool and pour it into a clean bottle with a tight-fitting lid.
6. Add distilled water (optional) if you would like to cut down on the sharp taste of strong herbs like ginger or mint and add them to your tinctures or teas later on.
7. Store in a dark place.

Extracting Herbs in Alcohol

These extracts are usually made with whole, fresh herbs but can be made with dried ones if they're more easily available. These extracts are great for adding to tinctures and teas and being ingested in their own right.

1. Chop the herb into manageable pieces and pour into a container with alcohol.
2. Let it soak for three days at least; overnight is great and more than that may start to make your finished product taste funny.
3. Strain the herbs out using a strainer, cheesecloth or other method.
4. Let the liquid cool and pour it into a clean bottle with a tight-fitting lid.
5. Add distilled water (optional) if you would like to cut down on the sharp taste of strong herbs like ginger or mint and add them to your tinctures or teas later on.
6. Store in a dark place.

Extracting Herbs in Glycerin

These extracts are usually made with fresh herbs but can be made with dried ones if they're more readily available. These extracts are great for adding to tinctures and teas and being ingested in their own right.

1. Chop the herb into manageable pieces.
2. Mix the herbs into glycerin by using a spoon, hand blender, or another mixing method until well combined.
3. Let it soak for at least one day; overnight is fine and more than that is better.
4. Strain the herbs out using a strainer, cheesecloth or another method.
5. Let the liquid cool off and pour it into a clean bottle with a tight-fitting lid.

6. Add distilled water (optional) if you would like to cut down on the sharp taste of strong herbs like ginger or mint and add them to your tinctures or teas later on.
7. Store in a dark place.

Extracting Herbs in Honey

These extracts are made with dried herbs that have been soaked and strained before adding them to the honey. These are great for adding to tinctures and teas and can also be ingested in their own right if they're diluted properly.

1. Boil water (or use distilled water) and pour over dried herbs in a jar or other container.
2. Cover and let sit at least overnight; more is better if you want to make a stronger extract.
3. Strain out herbs using a strainer, cheesecloth, or another method of straining.
4. Add honey to the herbs and stir thoroughly until well combined.
5. Let sit for several days; overnight is fine and more than that is better.
6. Strain out herbs using a strainer, cheesecloth, or other method of straining and pour into a clean glass bottle with a tight-fitting lid.
7. Add distilled water (optional) if you would like to cut down on the sharp taste of strong herbs like ginger or mint and add them to your tinctures or teas later on.
8. Store in a dark place.

Homemade Tinctures/Infusions

These extracts are made from dried herbs with a high alcohol content, usually 80 proof. This gives them a strong, potent flavor that is not so sweet and can be used for infusions, tinctures, baths, etc.

1. Place your dried herb into a jar and cover it with alcohol.
2. Let sit for two weeks to an hour before using or longer if you'd like the extraction to be even stronger.
3. Strain out the herbs and store them in a clean glass jar with a tight-fitting lid in a dark place.

Extracting Herbs in Vinegar

These extracts are made with dried herbs that have been soaked and strained before adding them to the vinegar. These are great for adding to tinctures and teas as well as being ingested in their own right.

1. Chop the herb into manageable pieces.
2. Add vinegar to your jar/bottle/container and cover, leaving at least one inch of airspace in between your herb and the vinegar so that it can infuse properly but not be lost when you strain out the herbs.
3. Let sit for at least one hour; overnight is great but less is just fine.
4. Strain out the herbs using a strainer, cheesecloth or another method of straining and pour into a clean glass jar with a tight-fitting lid in a dark place.
5. Add distilled water (optional) if you would like to cut down on the sharp taste of strong herbs like ginger or mint and add them to your tinctures or teas later on.
6. Store in a dark place.

Want to make extracts that are strong and potent but not necessarily candy-flavored? Try these methods and see what happens!

Percolation Extracts

You'll need to use a high percentage of alcohol for this type of extract, usually 80 proof. Soak your herbs in the alcohol and not let them dry out. Then strain the herbs out using a strainer, cheesecloth, or straining method and pour into a clean glass jar with a tight-fitting lid in a dark place.

Let it sit for several days; overnight is fine but more than that is better.

Strain out the herbs using a strainer, cheesecloth, or straining method and pour into a clean glass jar with a tight-fitting lid in a dark place.

Let it sit for several days; overnight is fine but more than that is better.

Strain out the herbs using a strainer, cheesecloth, or other straining method and pour into a clean glass jar with a tight-fitting lid in a dark place.

Let it sit for several days; overnight is fine but more than that is better.

Strain out the herbs using a strainer, cheesecloth, or straining method and pour into a clean glass jar with a tight-fitting lid in a dark place.

Let it sit for several days; overnight is fine but more than that is better.

There are many different ways you can use these types of extracts but the basic idea is to let them sit for several weeks until they build up in strength to be used in tinctures, teas, or infusions.

Fluid Extracts

This type of extract is very different from an herbal extract. It's a way to add potency to your tinctures and teas without having the herbs change color, go bad, and slowly lose flavor. The alcohol is usually less than 80 proof, such as vodka or absinthe.

You'll need a wide-mouth glass jar for this process and you'll also need to have some sort of immersion blender (such as an immersion blender or stick blender) that can be submerged a few inches into the mixture.

The glass jar should have a lid and then be filled with herbs, alcohol, water, or vinegar. As you add more liquid to fill up to about an inch from the top of the container (leaving room for shaking), use your immersion blender at low speed so that it doesn't splash out. Blend until all of the ingredients are mixed well and you have a nice, slightly frothy mixture that is potent but not too thick.

Combine the herbs in your jar with the alcohol (vodka or absinthe), water, vinegar, to taste. Blend on low speed until combined without splashing out of the container. The best way to do this is to use a blender (or a stick blender) that can be submerged a few inches into the mixture.

The glass jar should have a lid and then be filled with herbs, alcohol (vodka or absinthe), water, vinegar, to taste. As you add more liquid to fill up to about an inch from the top of the container (leaving room for shaking), use your immersion blender at low speed so that it doesn't splash out. Blend until all of the ingredients are mixed well and you have a nice slightly frothy mixture that is potent but not too thick.

Blend on low speed until combined without splashing out of the container. The best way to do this is to use a blender (or stick hand-blender) that can be submerged a few inches into the mixture.

Soxhlet Extracts

Another way to make a tincture is via the Soxhlet method (named Friedrich Soxhlet, who developed it in 1879). This technique requires more equipment and time but can result in a much stronger concentration of extracted constituents. Using ethanol as the solvent, place dried or fresh plant material into an extraction chamber with water. Attach an extractor tube that extends below the liquid level so that you can easily remove all liquids from this container by gravity feed without having to worry about siphoning any solid components back up into your mixture. Connect a condenser tube at the top of this apparatus which will capture and re-condense vaporized alcohol coming off during distillation; attach some type of collection device below the condenser to collect liquid products.

In a boiling water bath or double-boiler, heat distilled water and plant material in an extraction chamber until it boils for about 20 minutes. Then remove from heat while still hot, add more boiled water (to maintain that level), cover with a lid or other sealable device so as not to lose steam pressure under reduced atmospheric pressure during distillation process; wait 30-60 hours at room temperature before returning to this container and removing contents by gravity feed without siphoning any solid constituents back into your mixture; also attach some type of collection device below the condenser tube where you will be collecting liquid product

Continue writing the next sentences of long-form content: This was when I realized
that the company's herbals are potent.

I began using their herbs which were recommended to me by a friend and realized that they work on my health in ways I didn't know herbs could. They have so many different healing properties! My favorite is Tulsi because it improves digestion and helps with respiratory problems like asthma or bronchitis."

Flower essences are the most popular home remedies for anxiety. These remedies were founded by Edward Bach, a homeopath in England during the early 1900s, who was fascinated with the idea that flowers had healing properties. He did not believe in chemical medicine and even said that "in letting nature take its course we are letting God take his." He aimed to find a way to heal people without using the medicine, which he believed led to a dependency on more and more drugs.

He found that when he placed a flower in a bowl of water and allowed it to sit overnight, the flower's energy would infuse the water. When taken internally, this water could treat what he called a "specific condition", such as fear or guilt.

A few drops of these flower essences are usually taken under the tongue four times daily (or as directed by an herbalist). They are supposed to change our vibration from fear to love through their unique vibrational frequencies.

Some people who experience synesthesia and experiencing the sense of a different color when they hear sounds also see colored shapes and forms or get numbers as sounds. Others might have what is referred to as "visual sound," where they see words or words blend while reading them.

Synesthetes often develop synesthesia later in life and are highly intelligent and creative individuals who can even use their unique abilities to help them solve puzzles. Synesthetes also tend to have an excellent imagination and an affinity for art.

Aromatherapy is the use of certain plant essences as medicine through their scent. These are also known as essential oils and are extracted using either distillation or expression. The word "aromatherapy" is a combination of the Greek word for aroma, "aroma," and the French word for therapy, "therapies."

Distillation involves steeping a plant in water and collecting its components that evaporate, which can then be used to make the essential oils. The distillation process is extremely time-consuming and expensive but is the most effective way of extracting essential oils.

The expression uses steam to extract the resin from the plant, which is then pressed and dried for storage. The concept behind the expression is very similar to that of distillation – where the plant's essence (essence meaning life force) is released into the steam so it can be collected and used.

If you suspect you might have some form of synesthesia or a sense of color, sound, etc.

Chapter 5: Topical Preparations

For topical preparations, you'll need to mix the herbs into a tincture or oil and then apply it directly to the skin or use it in any type of bath preparation. These can be used for external use or internal use.

You can even make an herbal massage oil by combining the herbs, oil, and carrier oils.

Oil Based Extractions

These are combinations of oils and herbs used as topical preparations and usually found in the form of a balm or salve. They're usually rubbed onto the skin but can also be added to bath water for external use.

There are three main ways you can make these:

1. Combining ingredients and heating them together in a double boiler, on a stove, or in a microwave until they're melted together into an oil.

2. Combining ingredients and pouring the mixture into an oil-based container, such as a plastic or glass container, placing it in the fridge for at least 1 hour, removing it from the fridge and letting it sit on a counter until you're ready to use it. Then apply directly to the skin or mix it with a carrier oil like olive oil and use as a massage oil.

3. By combining ingredients and placing them into an oil-based container, such as a plastic or glass container, placing it in your fridge/freezer for at least 1 hour, removing it from the fridge/freezer and letting it sit on a counter until you're ready to use it. Then apply directly to the skin or mix it with a carrier oil like olive oil and use as a massage oil.

Topical Applications

These are a great addition to your herbal medicine cabinet because there are so many ways you can use them. Some of these are very common and used daily while others are more obscure but worth trying out.

The basic idea is this: herbs can be added to an oil, salve, balm, or other topical preparation to promote health in the body by applying it directly to the skin.

Here are some of the most common topical applications:

Essential oils can also be used topically. The essential oil is applied to the skin by pouring it into a carrier oil (such as olive oil), adding essential oils as needed, and using it to the skin. Essential oils are applied in many different ways: You can squeeze them onto your finger and rub them into the skin; You can mix them with a carrier oil, such as olive oil, and apply directly to the skin.

Essential oils can also be used to infuse an oil or salve. This is a mixture of herbs, essential oils, and carrier oil that is added to an oil or salve.

Local Applications

Local Applications are herbal medicines used to treat a specific area of the body such as the head or neck.

Several applications can be used for local applications but one, in particular, stands out: Joint Pain and Body Ache Plant Remedies ("Prunella vulgaris")

There are several ways you can use these remedies, all of which involve mixing it with an oil to make an oil salve. You can apply the oil directly to the skin, use it in a bath for bath applications, or mix it with a carrier oil and apply directly (this is more common in Europe than North America but it works great.

Chapter 6: Other Preparations

There are many other ways you can prepare your herbs to make them safer, more palatable, and more effective.

Concentrates

Concentrates are ways to use herbs with a high concentration of active ingredients that can be used in various ways. You can take them by the spoonful to ease a digestive problem or reduce an infection, take them via tincture in a bath, or even add them into your tea.

These concentrates are made using the following methods:

Infusions and Decoctions

Infusions are herbal preparations made with hot water and dried herbs, while decoctions are herbal preparations made with hot water and fresh herbs. These are great because they can be used in several different ways. They can be shaken into a tincture, boiled down and added to a bath, or even added into tea (for a chai twist, add some cloves and cinnamon sticks to your tea).

Lozenges

These are a type of oral preparation. They are made by mixing herbs with liquid glycerin so that it thickens into a paste. They're usually used in the mouth to relieve pain or as a mouthwash to clean out the mouth. There's also an external application and internal application which both work in different ways.

You can also make tinctures or infusions, then add them to an oil or liquid glycerin as a tablet. You can also put these in a large jar and get several ounces of the mixture for each ounce of herbs used.

There are many ways to prepare herbs in China. The most common methods involve using a tea ball or bags (similar to a tea bag but usually more extensive). These are usually made with either raw herbs or heated herbs.

These bags and balls can be used in two ways: They can be steeped in hot water for several minutes until the water turns herbal-colored, then they're strained out and used as an infusion. They can also be boiled in hot water and then used as an extract.

Other methods involve steeping the herbs in water using a special ceramic tea utensil and then straining the liquid out using a piece of cloth or your fingers. Some traditional herbalists also use bamboo baskets filled with hot water and herb trays to make herbal tea.

Chapter 7: Designing Herbal Formulas and Using Herbs Effectively

Mixing herbs is an essential part of herbalism, especially if you're trying to create healing mixtures for yourself or a loved one.
When you're creating a blend of herbs, it's important to remember that different herbs work as whole plants and not just isolated extracts. You may be taking a tincture or other form of an extract from an herb, but that's just the tip of the iceberg; for the herb to be effective, the rest of the plant is also needed. That's why a common saying used in herbalism is "form follows function." This means that the way a herb looks and feels on the plant (or in its complete form) affects how it behaves when ingested. In other words, you don't just take a tonic or tea; instead, you mix the essential oils and parts of the plant so that they work together. When you do this, both your container and your body become more efficient at using what you put into it.

In this chapter, we'll be looking at some of the basics of mixing herbs and creating herbal formulas. There's a lot to learn about herbs and blending them but once you understand these foundational concepts, you'll be able to mix herbs like a pro to heal yourself or take care of your loved ones.

When you're mixing herbs, you can create a "combination" (a mixture) or a "syrup" (an extract). A combination is created when you put the components of two or more ingredients together in a jar and mix them well. The combination allows the individual ingredients to mix and influence one another, so similar ingredients are used in formulas. A syrup is created when a liquid (lye) is poured over the herbs at home and stirred to activate them. Since the herbs have already been picked and dried, they don't need to be mixed with anything.

Many people like to create formulas using oils as well, but it's not necessary. You can create herbal formulas with just concentrated extracts mixed and most people use an oil in their blends because it enhances their properties and brings out their uniqueness. It's possible that you could become addicted to oils' effects so that you end up using them instead of your formulas. This is especially true for aromatic oils, which enhance the smell of a particular blend.

When you're creating a formula, it's important to remember that different herbs work as whole plants and not just isolated extracts. You may be taking a tincture or other form of an extract from an herb but that's just the tip of the iceberg; for the herb to be effective, the rest of the plant is also needed. That's why a common saying used in herbalism is "form follows function.

You can create a formula by putting the ingredients in a jar and mixing them well to blend. An alternative way of creating a formula is to dilute the herbs in a liquid like vinegar or grain alcohol, which preserves them for a longer period of time. Vinegar can be used to preserve your herbs when you don't have access to an herbalist who will do it for you. Vinegar is created by using natural bacteria that consume the sugars in fruit and turn them into acetic acid, which is what vinegar tastes like.

Conclusion

There is a lot of new information to take when you first start looking into herbalism and even more information to absorb once you've decided to start practicing. Luckily, it's easy for anyone to get started with herbalism and the best way to do this is by using the main practices and methods available.

This book has given you a lot of options but now the choice is up to you. Try out a few of these methods that look interesting and set aside time each day to keep up with them. In just a few weeks, you will see results and be on your way to becoming a fully-fledged herbalist.

You can then take this knowledge and apply it to your life and the lives of those around you.

A herbalist needs to know plenty of things before they get started with their journey and they should know most of them before they even start. This book has given you some great tips to get started, but there are many suggestions that we have not covered in this book.

BOOK 3

Natural Herbal Remedies

Introduction

Have you ever wondered what plants do for us? Or why should we care about them beyond their aesthetic appeal?
The answer is simple. Plants are the foundation of life as we know it. They grow and bear fruit; they provide the air we breathe, the water that sustains us, and many medicines that heal us. And because polluted air and dirty water threaten our wellbeing even more, today than ever before, plant knowledge is now more critical than ever.

Science has proven that certain plants are suitable for healing ulcers, rheumatism, malignant tumors, and many other common ailments. You can find plenty of these medicinal plants in your neighborhood or even in your own household. Most of these medicinal herbs are even easily grown in your backyard.
Some of them are so common that you can buy them at a grocery store or hardware store. Others are extremely rare and expensive.
For centuries families have used herbal remedies to heal common childhood diseases such as measles, mumps, and chickenpox. When American doctors were practically powerless against many of these illnesses, many parents turned to herbal remedies that had been proven effective in helping reduce the symptoms associated with these contagious diseases.
Nowadays, you may be more informed about how to protect your child from a variety of common, and not so common, illnesses than you were years ago. But, are you aware of which plants make good natural herbal remedies for a child's health? The older generations were well acquainted with them. Their forefathers had passed the knowledge of these herbs down from one generation to another for many centuries. And this information was written down and documented, in some cases, as early as the first half of the fourteenth century.

This book contains information about what plants do for us, how they help heal us, and how they can protect our health. Written by a certified naturopathic doctor, it explains the health benefits of medicinal herbs, the healing properties of plants, and how common diseases can be prevented.

This book contains recipe remedies for various illnesses. These remedies do not cure the illness, but they help you, the patient, recover faster.

When you use these recipe remedies, they are highly beneficial for your health. You get faster healing time and may not have to take long hospital stays. But when used along with modern medicine or self-help programs, you may be able to heal almost totally on your own with just a few weeks of herbal healing.
Enjoy this book and use this information wisely!

The Health Benefits of Natural Herbs

Native Americans are well known for their unwavering respect for nature, especially plants, which they consider sacred. They have a deep sense of kinship with the earth and all of its creatures; they were, after all, born of the earth. Their religions are deeply rooted in nature and the different natural elements. There is nothing that ties us to nature more than herbal medicine. Herbs have been known to be used as medicine for centuries upon centuries, and the use of herbs is not something that was left behind with the Native American way; it is still present today.

What Native Americans use as herbal remedies are not only helpful to them, but also to those who want to learn how to make their herb remedies. Native Americans have made great strides in the use of herbs. Nowadays they are considered one of the most knowledgeable groups of people when it comes to using natural medicine, and many people look up to them for guidance.

The art of using herbs as medicine can be described as an alliance between the body and nature's gifts. This natural form of healing is said to have numerous health benefits, and it does not involve the use of any harmful chemicals. It only relies on the healing properties found in nature itself. The fact that Native Americans have used medicinal plants for centuries already has proven that they can really heal diseases and ailments.

The Healing Properties Of Plants

Plants are organisms just like you and me, but with one major difference: they do not contain any nervous system or brain to process information about the environment. The human body does that for us, and the nervous system regulates many of our functions.

For instance, the human brain can memorize new data by using the information collected in previous lessons. The ability to memorize data is also similar to how plants process information from their environment. Plants seem to gather and store information about their surroundings like how humans use their brains to recognize patterns to help them make decisions about how they should behave or react in certain situations.

To make this clearer, let us say that a plant is growing on the side of a cliff. This plant, in two weeks, has experienced strong winds and extreme heat. The information gathered from these experiences made it decide to grow towards the wall to protect itself from strong winds and decrease its exposure to harsh sunlight. That is an example of how plants process their surroundings to adapt to the current conditions.

It is very similar to how humans process information about their surrounding environment. Humans rely on their senses of sight, smell, touch, and hearing to find out what is happening in their environment. In a way, we gather knowledge and information about our environment by using our senses.

Thus, as humans, it is logical to conclude that we are not much different from how plants sense their world.

Herbal Remedies for Your Child's Health

When it comes to your children's health, you need to know that there are a lot of things that you should be aware of. This chapter will discuss how you can keep your children protected against illness and illness-causing germs and bacteria. Keep in mind that it is very easy for a child to get sick especially when they are young since their immune system is not fully developed yet.

There are a lot of ways that you can keep your children as healthy as possible. You may want to consider the following ways to help their immune system work much better:

You should ensure that your child is given plenty of rest and sleep. It will make a huge difference in their overall health, growth, and development if they get sufficient rest each day. Getting enough sleep also helps improve one's immune system since it allows the body to be fully restored with energy and protect against illness.

One of the best things you can do for your child's safety is to keep them away from germs and bacteria. Ensure that you wash their hands frequently and always teach them not to touch their mouth with their hands. You should also make sure that they are not sharing anything with others, particularly food as it could get contaminated. If they have colds, it would be a good idea to make sure that they are taking medicine or going to the doctor.

You should also make sure that they play outside with friends as opposed to playing video games indoors. When the weather is nice, you should make sure to let them go out and play outdoors. This will help them socialize and interact with other people who will keep their immune systems healthy. You should also consider taking your children to a health spa when it is cold because this can help improve their energy levels.

You should make sure that you get your children vaccinated. When it comes to young children, this is very important since they are still very susceptible to many diseases. Some of the diseases they could contract include rashes, measles, chickenpox, meningitis, and type 1 diabetes.

The first three of these diseases can cause quite a lot of harm especially for small children so it is important to protect against them by giving them proper vaccinations.

The first vaccination that should be given is a triple vaccine, which protects against three diseases. The second vaccine is a combination vaccine and the third one is the meningitis C injection. In most cases, this is enough to help protect your child from these diseases.

It would also be best if you give your children plenty of exercises regularly. That will prevent them from becoming overweight and it will also make their immune system stronger.
We will discuss Herbal remedies that will help your child's immune system stay in tip-top shape!

1. Echinacea (E. Purpurea)

This herb has been used for centuries to treat a wide range of illnesses. In ancient times, it was known as one of nature's most powerful antibiotics. It is believed to stimulate the immune system and help boost its effectiveness in fighting infection.
Echinacea can be taken in liquid form and is most effective when used fresh rather than dry. It should be taken daily for up to 6 months when an immune-boosting remedy is required for best results.

2. Elderberry

This is one of the best natural remedies for colds and flu. Studies have shown that it is effective against a wide range of viruses. For best results, take the elderberry syrup daily during cold and flu season. After six months you can discontinue use as long as symptoms don't frequently recur (when used at appropriate concentration).

3. Garlic

Garlic is an excellent natural remedy for preventing colds, especially during cold and flu season. It has many other benefits as well. Garlic is also an immune stimulant and anti-inflammatory agent. You can take it in capsule form or fresh garlic juice.

4. Ginger

Ginger (Zingiber officinale) has been used as a medicinal herb for centuries to treat a wide range of ailments such as migraines, sore throats, indigestion, nausea, and the common cold.

For Children of 0-2 month

1. Newborn Dill [Anethum graveolens]

This is good for soothing the stomach and its strong anti-inflammatory action promotes fast recovery from ulcers. The same action is seen in ginger. It also has antimicrobial action on bacteria and viruses. Its main active ingredient is anethole which acts as a powerful anti-carcinogen, anti-biotic, anti-fungal, and antiviral agent.

2. Lavender [Lavandula angustifolia]

Lavender is a very beautiful plant that is widely used in decoration. It has several uses. Its main active ingredients are linalool (a strong antiseptic), linalyl acetate (a potent antimicrobial agent), Lavandula (another natural antibacterial agent), and linalyl formate (which has bactericidal effects).

3. Roman Chamomile [Chamaemelum nobile]

The main use of this herb is in the treatment of anxiety and depression. It is also good for stomach ulcers and, like dill, it acts as a great anti-inflammatory agent. It has the same actions as Lavender and Ginger, but with a stronger antibacterial effect.

4. Yarrow Achillea millefolium

This herb acts as a powerful anti-carcinogen, anti-biotic, anti-fungal, and antiviral agent. Its active ingredient is yarrow. It can be taken as a capsule or in fresh juice.

5. Elder [Sambucus nigra]

Elder has been used for centuries in traditional medicine. It is now known to have numerous health benefits including its antimicrobial solid action against bacteria, viruses, fungi, and yeasts.

For Children of 2-12 Months

1. Geranium [Pelargonium Graveolens]

It is good for the stomach, intestines, and lungs. It also helps in improving the immune system. Take Geranium as a herb or as an infusion.

2. Tangerine/Mandarin [Citrus reticulata]

The main effect of this herb is to stimulate the immune system. It does not act as a strong antibacterial agent although it has some anti-bacterial effects. Nevertheless, a lot of quotes have been made comparing it to lemon water. It can be used in capsules or taken in fresh juice.

3. Eucalyptus [Eucalyptus globules]

It is a very effective anti-bacterial and antifungal agent. It is also an antiviral and antiparasitic agent. It can be taken in the form of capsules or fresh juice.

4. Tea Tree [Melaleuca alternifolia]

Tea tree is a very well-known anti-bacterial, anti-fungal, and antiviral agent. It can be taken in the form of capsules or in fresh juice.

For Children of 12 Months-5 Years

1. Palmarosa [Cymbopogon martinii]

This herb is good for the lungs, the spleen, and the liver. It also acts as an anti-cancer agent. It can be taken in capsules or fresh juice.

For Children of 5 Years to 12 Years

1. Clary Sage [Salvia sclarea]

Clary Sage is good for the nervous system, especially the eyes and ears. It is also used in the treatment of liver disorders. Its active ingredients are linalyl acetate, linalool, eugenol (which acts as an antibacterial agent), and beta-caryophyllene (which has antifungal properties).

2. Nutmeg [Myristica fragrans]

This herb is particularly effective against respiratory and digestive tract infections. It is also known to help reduce nausea, vomiting, and diarrhea.

Aging

We all want to live to a ripe old age without looking a day over twenty-nine! Well, that's a lot easier said than done. The truth is, growing old is inevitable and so is the accompanying list of issues that show up as we age.

Aging can have a dramatic effect on our appearance, libido, and even our overall health. Stress, environmental toxins, and smoking all take their toll on our bodies over time, often resulting in illness (hence the need for herbal remedies).

Several herbs function as antioxidants, which effectively eliminate free radicals.

Herbal Allies:

- Ginkgo biloba
- Ginger
- Elderberries
- Horsetail
- Parsley
- Milk thistle
- Black currants

Anti-Aging Tea 1

- ½ cup Ginkgo biloba tea
- ½ cup ginseng tea

1. Combine the ingredients.
2. Take one-third of a cup three times daily.

Ginkgo is known to improve memory, while ginseng can boost energy levels.

Anti Aging Tea 2

- 12 drops goldenseal tincture
- 1 cup warm water
- Eight drops ginger root tincture
- 5 drops of cayenne tincture
- 30 drops burdock tincture
- ½ cup slippery elm tea

1. Combine all ingredients.
2. Take 2 to 3 tablespoons three times per day to improve circulation.

Asthma

Relevant tissue states: tension (constriction), dryness
Relevant herbal actions: anti-inflammatory, demulcent, expectorant, relaxant

Herbal Allies:

- ➢ Elecampane root
- ➢ Fennel seed
- ➢ Licorice root
- ➢ Marshmallow
- ➢ Mullein leaf

Though some herbs can interrupt an acute asthma attack, they are not covered in this book. The herbs and remedies mentioned here restore lung health over time and reduce chronic asthma symptoms. To observe the effects of these remedies, do breathing exercises before and after you take the herbs. A simple exercise is square breathing: Breathe in, hold, breathe out, and hold again, counting to four during each step. Cycle through 10 times. This builds resilience in the lungs—and works even better when paired with herbs!

Lung-Strengthening Tea

Makes 2¼ cups dried herb mix (enough for 14 to 18 quarts of tea)
The herbs here relax the lungs and induce the mucous membranes to release a little more fluid, soothing the racking dry cough. They also reduce inflammation in the lungs and, if there is any mucus present, help expectorate it. Drink a quart or more every day.

- 1 cup dried mullein leaf
- ½ cup fennel seed
- ½ cup dried marshmallow leaf
- ¼ cup dried licorice root

1. In a medium bowl, mix all the herbs. Store in an airtight container.
2. Make a hot infusion: Prepare a kettle of boiling water. Measure 2 to 3 tablespoons of herbs per quart of water and place in a mason jar or French press. Pour in the boiling water, cover, and steep for 20 minutes or until cool enough to drink.

Lung-Strengthening Tincture

Makes four fluid ounces (60 to 120 doses)
Elecampane is a strong lung stimulant; paired with relaxant mullein and soothing sweet licorice, it builds up weak lungs and protects against infection, to which asthmatics are more susceptible.

- 2 fluid ounces tincture of mullein
- 1 fluid ounce tincture of elecampane
- 1 fluid ounce tincture of licorice

1. In a small bottle, combine the tinctures. Cap the bottle and label it.
2. Take 1 to 2 droppersful 3 to 5 times per day.

Stress

Increased heart rate, elevated blood pressure, muscle tension, irritability, depression, stomachache, and indigestion are all signs of stress. To many people, stress means emotional stress. But stress can also be physical (such as the injuries that occur because of a car accident or surgery) and biochemical (including exposure to pesticides or pollution and even poor nutrition). These (and other causes) make the body produce increased amounts of adrenaline. This is how the body copes with stress. But the adrenaline release also causes the heart rate to increase, blood pressure to rise, and muscles to tense.

A host of conditions can develop when the body is subjected to prolonged stress. These include an increased rate of aging, reduced resistance to infection, weakened immune function (which, in turn, can lead to other conditions such as chronic fatigue syndrome), and hormone overproduction (which can lead to adrenal fatigue).
The best tool to fight off the effects of stress is a well-balanced diet and lifestyle.

Relevant tissue states: heat (agitation), tension
Relevant herbal actions: adaptogen, nervine, relaxant, sedative

Herbal Allies:

- Ashwagandha root
- Betony leaf and flower
- Catnip leaf and flower
- Chamomile flower
- Elderflower

- Ginger
- Goldenrod leaf and flower
- Hops
- Kava Kava
- Linden leaf and flower
- Peppermint
- Pleurisy
- Rose
- Sage leaf
- Skullcap
- St. John's wort leaf and flower
- Tulsi leaf
- Valerian

Everyone's stress is the same, and everyone's stress is different. We all have the same physiological response to stress—racing heart, shallow breathing, narrowed focus, heightened cortisol and blood sugar. But we react to potential stressors differently—something that bothers one person might roll right off another's back. Whatever is stressing you, herbs can help both as a short-term rescue in the immediate moment and in the long-term to build more "nerve reserve" and poise in the face of difficulties.

Soothe Up! Tea

Makes 3¾ cups dried herb mix (enough for 22 to 30 quarts of tea)

This is the perfect mixture for those days when you feel like everything is falling all around you: just take a moment, make a cup, drink it as deliberately as you can, and let the warmth and relaxation move through you.

If your stress manifests with a feeling of heaviness and downtrodden exhaustion, include ¼ cup of dried goldenrod and/or sage.

If it shows up as digestive upsets, include ¼ cup of dried chamomile and/or catnip.

Drink a quart or more every day.

1 cup dried betony leaf and flower

1 cup dried tulsi leaf

½ cup dried linden leaf and flower

½ cup dried rose petals

½ cup dried elderflower

¼ cup St. John's wort leaf and flower dried

1.In a medium bowl, mix all the herbs. Store in an airtight container.

2.Make a hot infusion: Prepare a kettle of boiling water. Measure 2 to 3 tablespoons of herbs per quart of water and place in a mason jar or French press. Pour in the boiling water, cover, and steep for 20 minutes or until cool enough to drink.

TIP: Omit the St. John's wort if you are concurrently taking pharmaceuticals.

Calm Down Tea

1 teaspoon powdered ginger

1 teaspoon powdered valerian root

1 teaspoon powdered pleurisy root

2 cups boiling water

1. Combine the above herbs in a nonmetallic container and cover with boiling water; steep for 30 minutes; cool and strain.

2. Take one tablespoon at a time, as needed, up to two cups a day.

1 to 2 teaspoons peppermint leaves
1 teaspoon valerian root
1 cup boiling water

1. Combine the above ingredients and cover with the boiling water; steep for 20 to 30 minutes; strain.

2. Drink up to one cup per day, as needed.

Headache

Headaches are very common and can be dull and steady, stabbing, gnawing, or throbbing. There are many kinds of headaches with many different causes. Sometimes tension, fatigue, or stress can cause a headache. Problems with the eyes, ears, nose, throat, or teeth can bring on a headache, such as allergies, injuries, infections, tumors, and many diseases. Headaches are also big business. Americans spend more than $1 billion each year buying medicines to help combat headaches.

Most people take nonsteroidal anti-inflammatory drugs (NSAIDs) such as aspirin, ibuprofen, or indomethacin, or even stronger painkillers. But these drugs have unwanted, and sometimes serious, side effects, including ulcers and an increased tendency to bleeding. Herbs can offer a safer alternative.

Relevant tissue states: heat or cold, damp or dry, tense or lax
Relevant herbal actions: anodyne, anti-inflammatory, astringent, circulatory stimulant, relaxant

Herbal Allies:

- Betony leaf and flower
- Catnip
- Chamomile flower

- Feverfew
- Peppermint
- Pleurisy root
- White Willow
- Wintergreen
- Ginger
- Linden leaf and flower
- Marshmallow
- Meadowsweet flower
- Sage leaf
- Tulsi leaf
- Wild lettuce

Headaches arise from a variety of imbalances. Some are simple one-off causes—dehydration, sleep debt, dietary excesses, alcohol, caffeine, medications. For those, you want quick pain relief while you supply what's missing or simply wait for the body to recover. (When unsure of where to start, turn to betony.)

For long-term relief, it's important to identify your triggers, as well as the underlying patterns that contribute to your pain; this takes some experimentation. The following herbal remedies are designed to address the most common types of headaches we see, but try different combinations of herbs to refine the remedy and make it as personal as possible. If you have recurrent headaches and find this helps, drink a quart or more daily as a preventive.

Cooling Headache Tea

Makes 3¼ cups dried herb mix (enough for 22 to 28 quarts of tea)

If a headache makes you turn red-faced, and the pain feels hot, sharp, and very sensitive to the touch, this is for you. This kind of headache often results from tension, stress or anxiety, sinus congestion, or direct nerve pain. These herbs cool, relax (be aware the wild lettuce may make you sleepy), and drain.

1 cup dried betony leaf and flower
1 cup dried meadowsweet flower
½ cup dried linden leaf and flower
½ cup dried marshmallow leaf
¼ cup dried wild lettuce leaf and stalk

1. In a medium bowl, mix all the herbs. Store in an airtight container.

2. Make a hot infusion: Prepare a kettle of boiling water. Measure 2 to 3 Tablespoons of herbs per quart of water and place in a mason jar or French press. Pour in the boiling water, cover, and steep for 30 to 40 minutes. Drink warm or cool. One cup of this tea should begin to give some relief.

Warming Headache Tea

Makes 3¼ cups dried herb mix (enough for 22 to 28 quarts of tea)

If your headaches strike, you have a pale face and the pain feels cold, dull, and broad, try this blend. This type of headache is often caused by hypothyroidism, liver congestion, and circulatory stagnation. These herbs warm, gently astringe, and improve circulation. (If caffeine usually works as a headache remedy for you, try this.) If you have recurrent headaches and find this helps, drink a quart or more daily as a preventive.

1 cup dried betony leaf and flower
1 cup dried tulsi leaf
½ cup dried chamomile flower
½ cup dried sage leaf
¼ cup dried ginger

1. In a medium bowl, mix all the herbs. Store in an airtight container.

2. Make a hot infusion: Prepare a kettle of boiling water. Measure 2 to

3 tablespoons of herbs per quart of water and place in a mason jar or French press. Pour in the boiling water, cover, and steep for 30 to 40 minutes. Drink warm to hot. One cup of this tea should begin to give some relief.

Peppery Headache Tea

1 teaspoon feverfew leaves
1 teaspoon peppermint leaves
1 cup boiling water
Honey

1. Combine the above herbs in a nonmetallic container and cover with boiling water; steep for 30 minutes; strain.

2. Add honey to taste. Take a tablespoon at a time, up to one cup a day.

Hangover

The hidden enemy in a night out with your friends is the notorious hangover. The day-after side effect of excessive alcohol intake can cause dehydration, irritability (due to the swings in the blood sugar levels), headache, stomach acid, and dizziness.

The enemy to fight is dehydration. Be sure to drink water during your night-out and before going to bed; it will make a recovery easier the day after.

Symptomatology:

- Inflammation
- Dehydration

Actions Required:

- Anti-inflammatory
- Emollient

Recommended Herbs:

- Catnip leaves
- Peppermint leaves
- Barberry leaves
- Heal-all leaves
- Oregon Grape root
- Goldenseal leaves
- Plantain leaves
- Calendula Flowers
- Chamomile Flowers
- Linden leaves
- Licorice root
- Ginger root
- St. John’s Wort leaves

- Marshmallow (leaves)

Hangover Tea 1

- 1 tsp Catnip dried leaves
- 1 tsp Peppermint dried leaves
- 1 tsp Barberry dried leaves
- 1 cup distilled boiling water

Directions:
Pour boiling water over the herbs mixture. Let rest for 30 minutes: strain and drink.

Hangover Tea 2

- 1 tsp Barberry dried leaves
- 1 tsp Heal-all dried leaves
- 1 tsp Oregon Grape root
- 1 cup distilled boiling water

Directions:
Pour boiling water over the herbs mixture. Let rest for half an hour. Strain and drink throughout the day

Hangover Tea 3

- 1 tsp Barberry dried leaves
- 1 tsp Goldenseal dried leaves
- 1 tsp Oregon Grape root
- 1 cup distilled boiling water

Directions:

Pour boiling water over the herbs mixture. Let rest for half an hour—strain and drink throughout the day.

Hangover Tea 4

- 1 tbsp. Plantain dried leaf
- 1 tbsp. Calendula dried flower
- 1 tbsp. Chamomile dried flower
- 1 tbsp. Dried linden leaves
- 1 tbsp. Licorice root
- 1 tbsp. Dried Ginger root
- 1 tbsp. Dried St. John's Wort leaves

Directions:
Mix the herbs in a mason jar for easy storage. Put 1 tbsp. of the mixture in 1 cup of distilled boiling water. Let rest for half an hour. Strain and drink throughout the day

Warning: Do not add St. John Wort if you are under pharmaceutics.

Hypertension

The list of circulatory disorders is almost endless and includes heart disease, strokes, hypertension, and atherosclerosis, to name a few. These and other circulatory conditions are the number-one cause of death in this country, killing nearly one million Americans every year. As we age, our body's ability to keep a proper equilibrium between blood clotting and blood liquefaction begins to go awry.

On the one hand, blood must clot if we are to keep from bleeding to death, yet, on the other hand, it must be free-flowing and liquid to travel easily through the body's blood vessels. The older we get, the "stickier" our blood gets, and our blood's ability to flow diminishes. When this occurs, the stage is set for blood clots, clogged arteries, strokes, and heart attacks.

Relevant tissue states: heat, tension
Relevant herbal actions: hypotensive, nervine, relaxant, sedative

Herbal Allies:

- Black Cohosh
- Black Currant
- Burdock
- Cayenne
- Dandelion
- Garlic
- Ginger
- Ginkgo Biloba
- Ginseng
- Goldenseal
- Gotu Kola
- Kelp
- Linden leaf and flower
- Marshmallow
- Raspberry

- Rose
- Slippery Elm
- Yarrow leaf and flower

Occasional high blood pressure is normal—it's a part of the natural response to stressful situations. Over time, though, high blood pressure can cause or worsen other cardiovascular problems. Herbs offer a nice suite of actions to reduce high blood pressure, often by addressing root causes rather than merely acting symptomatically.

It's worth noting that high blood pressure isn't always bad: New information indicates that hypertension that develops in the elder years may help reduce the risk of dementia.

Soft Hearted Tea

Makes 2 cups dried herb mix (enough for 12 to 16 quarts of tea)

Reducing stress makes a big difference, so herbs that can relax the mind while soothing the physical heart are ideal. For those with very dry constitutions, prepare this as a cold infusion instead. Drink a quart or more every day.

1 cup dried linden leaf and flower
½ cup dried marshmallow leaf
½ cup dried rose petals

1.In a small bowl, mix all the herbs. Store in an airtight container.

2. Make a hot infusion: Prepare a kettle of boiling water. Measure 2 to 3 tablespoons of herbs per quart of water and place in a mason jar or French press. Pour in the boiling water, cover, and steep for 20 minutes or until cool enough to drink.

Insomnia

Insomnia is any difficulty in sleeping. Some people find it difficult to fall asleep, while others can fall asleep easily but don't stay asleep. Nearly one-fourth of all Americans have an occasional problem sleeping, but some people (as much as 10 percent of the American population) have chronic insomnia. Insomnia can occur for many reasons, including stress and nervous tension, excessive intake of caffeinated drinks, and irregular sleeping habits.

Insomnia can lead to fatigue and an inability to function at an optimal energy level during the day. Irritability, daytime drowsiness, and memory impairment often affect those who have insomnia.

Relevant tissue states: heat (agitation), tension
Relevant herbal actions: hypnotic, relaxant, sedative

Herbal Allies:

- Ashwagandha root
- Betony leaf and flower
- Catnip leaf and flower
- Chamomile flower
- Hops
- Linden leaf and flower
- Passionflower
- Rose
- Valerian
- Wild lettuce

Wild animals don't have insomnia. Hikers in the wilds don't either. According to a 2013 study in the journal Current Biology, just a few days in an outdoor environment, with no artificial light exposure, is enough to reestablish normal circadian rhythms—even in people who are habitual "night owls" in their city lives. This tracks with a large and growing body of evidence that indicates that our electrically lit environments are directly responsible for most sleep disturbances we experience.

Reducing evening exposure to bright lights—including TV, computer, and smartphone screens—is one of the most important steps you can take to fight insomnia. Dimming lights and avoiding screens for at least an hour before bed, and taking the herbal remedies offered here, are sure ways to improve both the quantity and quality of your sleep.

End-Of-The-Day Elixir

Makes 4 fluid ounces (60 to 120 doses)

This blend of relaxants and gentle sedatives doesn't force sleep but helps relieve the tension, anxiety, and distraction that make it difficult to transition into sleep. This formula (and any herbs taken to aid in sleep) is best taken in "pulse doses," which is much more effective than taking thc total dosc all at oncc right at bedtime. It gives the herbs time to start working in your system and emphasizes to the body that it's time to transition into sleep.

1 fluid ounce tincture of chamomile
1 fluid ounce tincture of betony
¾ fluid ounce tincture of ashwagandha
½ fluid ounce tincture of catnip
½ fluid ounce tincture of linden
¼ fluid ounce honey (plain or rose petal–infused)

1.In a small bottle, combine the tinctures and honey. Cap the bottle and label it.
2.One hour before bedtime, take 1 to 2 drops.
3.Thirty minutes before bedtime, take another 1 to 2 drops.
4.At bedtime, take the final 1 to 2 drops.

Sleep! Formula

Makes 4 fluid ounces (60 to 120 doses)

For this formula, we recruit wild lettuce, the strongest hypnotic (sleep-inducing) herb in this book. This is especially helpful if part of what's keeping you up at night is physical pain, as wild lettuce also has a pain-relieving effect. This formula, like End-of-the-Day Elixir, is best taken in "pulse doses."

2 fluid ounces tincture of wild lettuce
1 fluid ounce tincture of betony
½ fluid ounce tincture of chamomile
½ fluid ounce tincture of linden

1.In a small bottle, combine the tinctures. Cap the bottle and label it.
2.One hour before bedtime, take 1 to 2 drops.
3.Thirty minutes before bedtime, take another 1 to 2 drops.
4.At bedtime, take the final 1 to 2 drops.

Insomnia Relief Tea

1 teaspoon chamomile flowers
1 teaspoon hops
1 teaspoon valerian root
1 cup boiling water

1. Combine the above herbs.
2. Take one tablespoon of the mixture and cover with the boiling water; let steep for 30 minutes; strain.
3. Drink warm, as needed, half a cup at a time.

Sweet Dreams Tea

2 teaspoons catnip leaves
1 teaspoon hops
2 teaspoons chamomile flower
2 teaspoons passionflower
1 cup boiling water

1. Combine the above herbs in a glass container; cover with boiling water; steep for 30 minutes; cool and strain.
2. Take one hour before bedtime.

Indigestion

This condition happens when you do not digest something you eat. It may be due to many causes: from eating too much or too fast to serious conditions such as intolerances, ulcers, or gastritis.

Symptomatology:

- Abdominal tension

Actions Required:

- Carminative
- Relaxant

Recommended Herbs:

- Licorice root
- Peppermint leaves
- Ginger root
- Angelica root
- Chamomile Flowers
- Black Cohosh root
- Fennel seeds
- Dandelion Root
- Sage Leaves

Digestive Tea 1

- 1 tsp Licorice root dried, powder
- 1 tsp Peppermint dried leaves
- 1 cup distilled boiling water

Directions:
Pour boiling water over the herbs. Let steep for 20 minutes. Strain and drink warm to help digestion.

Digestive Tea 2

- 1 tsp Ginger root dried
- 1 tsp Angelica root dried
- 1 tsp Chamomile dried flowers
- 1 tsp Peppermint dried leaves
- 1 cup distilled boiling water

Directions:
Pour boiling water over the herbs mixture. Let rest for half an hour: strain and drink.

Digestive Tea 3

- 1 tsp Black Cohosh root dried
- 1 tsp Angelica root dried
- 1 cup distilled boiling water

Directions:
Pour boiling water over the herbs mixture. Let rest for 30 minutes—strain and drink throughout the day to help with persistent indigestion.

Intestinal Gas Tincture

- 3 tbsp. Fennel seed tincture
- 3 tbsp. Ginger Root tincture
- 3 tbsp. Licorice Root tincture
- 3 tbsp. Peppermint tincture
- 3 tbsp. Chamomile Flowers tincture

Directions:
Put the tinctures in an amber glass bottle with a dropper lid in the indicated proportions. Label it. Take 5 drops after each meal.

Preventive Tincture

- 3 tbsp. Fennel seed tincture
- 3 tbsp. Dandelion Root tincture
- 3 tbsp. Licorice Root tincture
- 3 tbsp. Sage Leaves tincture

Directions:
Put the tinctures in an amber glass bottle with a dropper lid in the indicated proportions. Label it. Take 3 drops before each meal.

Menstrual Cycle Irregularities

The irregularities include various disruptions of the menstrual cycle. Each is addressed slightly differently, but a few overarching actions emerge that help with all of them: nourishing the body, improving circulation, and stimulating the liver and kidneys to clear away used-up hormones.

Delayed or absent menses may be due to a lack of adequate nourishment, especially protein, or disruptions in hormone levels. (Sometimes these share a cause. A high-sugar diet is nutrient-poor, and the havoc it wreaks on blood sugar levels has a cascade effect that disrupts hormone balance. Stress makes us tend to eat gratifying but poor-quality food, and excessive stress-response hormones interfere with the normal actions of estrogen and progesterone.)

Irregular cycles, with no predictable pattern, may also be due to poor nourishment, liver stagnation or strain, or an irregular lifestyle—especially erratic sleep habits. The daily cycle shapes the monthly cycle, like small and large gears interlocking in a watch.

Overheavy bleeding generally comes from hormones not clearing efficiently at the liver, though it may also be connected with the development of fibroids or polyps. If heavy bleeding persists, seek medical attention.

Finally, let's talk about the most common menstrual ailment: dysmenorrhea, or menstrual pain, which usually begins just before menstruation, may occur in the lower abdomen or the lower back (and sometimes even into the thighs). Other accompanying symptoms may include nausea, vomiting, headache, and either constipation or diarrhea. This condition affects more than half of all women.

There are two types of dysmenorrhea, primary and secondary. In primary dysmenorrhea, there is no underlying pain causing the disorder. It is thought that the pain occurs when uterine contractions reduce blood supply to the uterus. This may occur if the uterus is in the wrong position, if the cervical opening is narrow, and lack exercise.

Secondary dysmenorrhea is when the pain is caused by some gynecological disorder, such as endometriosis (when the endometrium, the tissue that lines the uterus, abnormally grows on surfaces of other structures in the abdominal cavity), adenomyosis (in-growth of the endometrium into the uterine musculature), lesions, inflammation of the fallopian tubes, or uterine fibroids. Uterine fibroids are tumors of the uterus that are not usually cancerous. Also known as myomas, these masses occur in nearly one-quarter of all women by forty. Some women with uterine fibroids may have no symptoms. However, if symptoms are present they include increased frequency of urination, a bloated feeling, pressure, pain, and abnormal bleeding.

Relevant tissue states: cold (stagnation), laxity
Relevant herbal actions: astringent, carminative, circulatory stimulant, emmenagogue, nutritive, rubefacient

Herbal Allies:

- Angelica
- Ashwagandha root
- Betony leaf and flower
- Black Cohosh
- Blue Vervain
- Chamomile flower
- Cramp Bark
- Dandelion leaf
- Elecampane
- Feverfew
- Ginger
- Goldenrod leaf and flower
- Kelp
- Marigold
- Milk thistle seed

- Nettle leaf
- Passionflower
- Peppermint
- Pulsatilla
- Raspberry
- Sage leaf
- Self-heal leaf and flower
- St. John's Wort
- Tulsi leaf

Steady Cycle Tea

Makes 3½ cups dried herb mix (enough for 20 to 28 quarts of tea)

These herbs provide substantial nourishment and a bit of gentle kidney, lymphatic, and endocrine stimulation. Long-term use of a formula like this has been the major factor in improving many of our clients with menstrual irregularities of all types. Add ginger if you run cold, betony if you're frequently anxious, and peppermint for taste (if you like it). Drink a quart or more every day.

1 cup dried nettle leaf
1 cup dried dandelion leaf
½ cup dried goldenrod leaf and flower
½ cup dried self-heal leaf and flower
¼ cup dried tulsi leaf
¼ cup dried kelp

1. In a small bowl, mix all the herbs. Store in an airtight container.
2. Make a long infusion: Prepare a kettle of boiling water. Measure 2 to 3 tablespoons of herbs per quart of water and place in a mason jar or French press. Pour in the boiling water, cover, and steep for 8 hours or overnight.

Bleed On! Tea

Makes 3 cups dried herb mix (enough for 20 to 26 quarts of tea)

To bring on menstruation, drink this tea for 3 days to 1 week before the expected start of your next period. Drink this tea very hot for best results. Reheat as necessary and drink a quart or more over the day. For a stronger effect, take a drop of angelica tincture together with each cup of tea.

1 cup dried chamomile flower
1 cup dried tulsi leaf
⅓ cup dried goldenrod leaf and flower
⅓ cup dried ginger
⅓ cup dried angelica root

1.In a small bowl, mix all the herbs. Store in an airtight container.

2.Make a hot infusion: Prepare a kettle of boiling water. Measure 2 to 3 tablespoons of herbs per quart of water and place in a mason jar or French press. Pour in the boiling water, cover, and steep for 20 minutes or until cool enough to drink.

Daily Soothing Menstrual Tea

2 teaspoons black haw root or bark
2 teaspoons passionflower
2 cups cold water

1. Combine the above herbs in a pan and cover with cold water; soak overnight; strain.
2. Take half a cup, up to four times daily.

Back Pain

Relevant tissue states: tension (spasms), heat (inflammation)
Relevant herbal actions: analgesic, anti-inflammatory, antispasmodic, relaxant

Herbal Allies:

- Ginger
- Goldenrod leaf and flower
- Meadowsweet flower
- Mullein root
- Solomon's seal root
- Wild lettuce

Back pain can have many causes—injury, spasms, sciatica (nerve pain), disc problems, and so on. The long-term resolution requires figuring out what exactly is the root of the problem, but in the meantime, these herbs and formulas will relieve pain and release tension, allowing you to move more freely.

Spine's Fine Tincture

Makes 4 fluid ounces (40 to 120 doses)
These warming, relaxant, analgesic herbs quell the spasms responsible for most back pain, regardless of whether the pain is acute or chronic, muscular or connective, etc. If you have infused oil made from fresh goldenrod or ginger, use it as massage oil after applying this formula topically. For help sleeping, take 1 to 4 dropperful of tincture of wild lettuce by mouth—this will also contribute more pain-relieving action.

- 1 fluid ounce tincturc of Solomon's seal
- 1 fluid ounce tincture of ginger
- ½ fluid ounce tincture of goldenrod
- ½ fluid ounce tincture of meadowsweet
- ½ fluid ounce tincture of mullein root (see Tip)

- ½ fluid ounce tincture of St. John's wort (optional; see Tip)

1. In a small bottle, combine the tinctures. Cap the bottle and label it.
2. Take 1 to 4 dropppersful by mouth 3 to 5 times per day.
3. Additionally, squirt 1 to 4 droppersful into your palm and rub it into the back muscles.

TIP: If the vertebral discs are impinged or worn away, increase the mullein root to 1 fluid ounce. It specifically supports these tissues. If sciatica or other radiating nerve pain is present, include St. John's wort (unless you are taking pharmaceuticals). It regenerates damaged nerve tissue.

Warming Compress

Makes 1 compress

This simple application provides immediate relief.

- 16 fluid ounces water
- ½ cup dried ginger (see Tip)
- ¼ cup Epsom salts

1. In a small pot with a tight-fitting lid over high heat, combine all the ingredients. Cover and bring to a boil. Reduce the heat and simmer for 5 minutes. Meanwhile, fill a hot water bottle.

2. Soak a cloth in the hot tea, holding it in a dry spot and letting it cool in the air until hot but comfortable to the touch.

3. Lie down and place the wet cloth over your back. Cover with a dry cloth and lay the hot water bottle on top. Get comfortable and let it soak in for 10 to 20 minutes. You should feel warmth, relaxation, and relief from pain.

4. Repeat as often as desired.

TIP: Have pain, but no dried ginger? If all you have on hand is fresh ginger from the grocery store, you can use that, too—sliced, chopped, or grated.

Bites and Stings

Relevant tissue states: heat (inflammation)
Relevant herbal actions: anti-inflammatory, astringent, lymphatic, immune stimulant

Herbal Allies:

- Peppermint leaf
- Plantain leaf
- Rose
- Self-heal leaf and flower
- Yarrow leaf and flower

Whether it's mosquitoes, black flies, or fire ants, most bug bites are fairly simple: We just need to reduce the inflammation. Bee and wasp stings are a bit more intense: Here, our goals include drawing out the venom, if possible, reducing inflammation, and helping the immune system cope with the venom that has entered the body. Watch for anaphylaxis! If someone stung or bitten is having difficulty breathing, seek help immediately.

Cooling Compress

Makes 1 compress
Peppermint's menthol provides a cooling sensation to the skin, while at the same time increasing blood circulation and dispersing the irritants from the bite or sting site.

- 16 fluid ounces water
- ½ cup dried peppermint leaf
- ¼ cup Epsom salts

1. In a small pot with a tight-fitting lid over high heat, combine all the ingredients. Cover and bring to a boil. Remove from the heat.
2. Soak a cloth in the hot tea, holding it in a dry spot and letting it cool in the air until hot but comfortable to the touch.

3. Apply the cloth to the bite or sting.
4.

Bug Bite Relief Spray

Makes 8 fluid ounces (number of applications varies by use)
If you regularly walk through clouds of mosquitoes or black flies or live in an area infested with chiggers, you'll want this cooling, itch-relieving spray stocked for when you come inside.

- 4 fluid ounces nonalcoholic witch hazel extract or apple cider vinegar
- 2 fluid ounces tincture of rose
- 1 fluid ounce tincture of self-heal
- 1 fluid ounce tincture of yarrow

1. In a bottle with a fine-mist sprayer top, combine all the ingredients. Cap the bottle and label it.
2. Liberally spray wherever you've been bitten.

Bloating

Relevant tissue states: dampness (stagnation)
Relevant herbal actions: carminative, lymphatic

Herbal Allies:

- Angelica
- Calendula flower
- Fennel seed
- Ginger
- Peppermint leaf
- Self-heal leaf and flower

Bloating may be extremely common, but it's not insignificant! When you become bloated, it's a buildup of gas in the bowels or a flood of fluid swelling in the lymphatic vessels wrapped around the intestines. Fennel and ginger are great for reducing gas, but for fluid bloating, you'll want lymphatic drainers such as calendula or self-heal.

Dispersing Infusion

Makes 3 to 3½ cups dried herb mix (enough for 18 to 24 quarts of tea)
This helps with bloating, no matter what kind. Feel free to adjust the proportions to your taste, and if you don't have every herb, it is still effective. Be forewarned: This will induce you to pass some gas!

- 1 cup dried calendula flower
- 1 cup dried self-heal leaf and flower
- ½ cup fennel seed
- ½ cup dried ginger
- ½ cup dried peppermint leaf (optional)

1. In a medium bowl, mix together all the herbs, including the peppermint (if using). Store in an airtight container.
2. Make a hot infusion: Prepare a kettle of boiling water. Measure 2 to 3 tablespoons of herbs per quart of water and place in a

mason jar or French press. Pour in the boiling water, cover, and steep for 20 minutes or until cool enough to drink.

3. Drink 1 to 2 teacups after meals to prevent or dispel bloating. If this is a chronic issue, drink a quart or more every day.

Dispersing Tincture

Makes 4 fluid ounces (60 to 120 doses)

A few squirts of this tincture blend will disperse gas and fluid bloating alike. Bring it with you the next time you head out for pizza or go to the local diner, and pass it around after the meal!

- 1 fluid ounce tincture of calendula
- 1 fluid ounce tincture of self-heal
- 1 fluid ounce tincture of fennel
- ½ fluid ounce tincture of ginger
- ½ fluid ounce tincture of angelica

1. In a small bottle, combine the tinctures. Cap the bottle and label it.
2. Take 1 to 2 droppersful as needed.

Bronchitis/Chest Cold/Pneumonia

Relevant tissue states: dampness, cold (depressed vitality)
Relevant herbal actions: antimicrobial, astringent, decongestant, diaphoretic, expectorant, pulmonary tonic

Herbal Allies:

- Angelica
- Elder
- Elecampane root
- Garlic
- Ginger
- Pine
- Sage leaf
- Thyme leaf

When you have a lung infection, don't suppress the cough, it's a vital response! Our goal is to cough when it's productive, so all the irritating or infectious material is expelled as you cough up phlegm and to reduce the amount of unproductive coughing. If you can't bring up the phlegm, you may find a simple cough developing into pneumonia because of the mucus buildup. (True pneumonia is a serious condition—seek higher care. Meanwhile, take elecampane and garlic—they're your strongest allies for this problem.)

Infection-instigated coughs are usually wet, and the herbs we discuss here assume that's the case. Refer to Cough for more help determining what kind of cough you have. The goal is to get it just a little on the moist side—nice and productive—so you can expel that phlegm.

As with any respiratory condition, herbal steam is a great remedy all on its own, combating infection and greatly improving blood circulation—which means immune activity—in the lungs. Simple steam with thyme or sage is very good for this problem.

Fire Cider

It makes about 1 quart

Traditional fire cider recipes are blends of spicy and aromatic stimulating expectorants that will heat you and help you get the gunk out. In this version, we sneak in some immune stimulants and a good source of vitamin C. *Do not consume this if you take pharmaceutical blood thinners.*

- 1 whole head garlic, cloves peeled and chopped
- 1 (2-inch) piece fresh ginger, chopped
- ¼ cup dried pine needles
- ¼ cup dried sage leaf
- ¼ cup dried thyme leaf
- ¼ cup dried elderberry
- ¼ cup dried rose hips
- 2 tablespoons dried elecampane root
- 2 tablespoons dried angelica root
- 1 quart apple cider vinegar
- Honey or water, for sweetening or diluting (optional)

1. In a quart-size mason jar, combine the garlic, ginger, and remaining herbs.
2. Fill the jar with the vinegar. Cover the jar with a plastic lid, or place a sheet of wax paper under the jar lid before you screw down the ring. (The coating on the bottom of metal mason jar lids corrodes when exposed to vinegar.)
3. Let the herbs macerate in the vinegar for 2 weeks or longer.
4. Strain, bottle, and label the finished fire cider. If the vinegar is too heating to be comfortable on your stomach, add some honey (up to one-fourth the total volume), or dilute your dose with water.
5. Take a shot (about ½ fluid ounce) at the first sign of mucus buildup in the lungs, and every couple hours thereafter until symptoms resolve.

Burns and Sunburn

Relevant tissue states: heat
Relevant herbal actions: anti-inflammatory, antimicrobial, antiseptic, vulnerary

Herbal Allies:

- Calendula flower
- Linden leaf and flower
- Marshmallow
- Peppermint leaf
- Plantain leaf
- Rose petals
- Self-heal leaf and flower

Immediately following a burn, run cold water over the area—the skin retains heat for much longer than you'd expect. (If blisters form in the burned area, be very gentle with them and don't break them before they naturally slough off, if you can avoid it.) Then, gently clean the wound, removing any dirt or contaminant. Apply the herbs, combining antiseptics to prevent infection with cooling, wound-healing herbs to encourage tissue regeneration.

Apply any of the herbal allies in a wash, compress, poultice, or infused honey—don't use oily preparations (like slaves) on burns because they trap the heat in the tissue.
Do not underestimate the power of a marshmallow root poultice! Simply saturate a handful of marshmallow root with enough cold water to make a gloopy mass and apply it to the burn. Cover with gauze and leave in place for 20 minutes. Repeat frequently.

Burn-Healing Honey

It makes about 1 pint
Honey is the single best healing agent for burns: If you have nothing but plain honey, you're still in good shape. It gets even better, though, when you infuse these healing herbs into it ahead of time.

- ½ cup fresh calendula flower
- ½ cup fresh rose petals
- 1 pint honey, gently warmed

1. Put the calendula and rose petals in a pint-size mason jar.
2. Fill the jar with warm honey. Seal the jar and place it in a warm area to infuse for 1 month.
3. In a double boiler, gently warm the closed jar until the honey has a liquid consistency. Strain the infused honey into a new jar, pressing the marc against the strainer to express as much honey as you can.
4. After cooling and cleaning a burn site, apply a layer of the infused honey and cover lightly with a gauze bandage. Refresh the application at least twice a day.

Sunburn Spray

Makes 8 fluid ounces
A few spritzes cool the skin and begin to reduce inflammation.

- 1 tablespoon dried peppermint leaf
- 1 tablespoon dried plantain leaf
- 1 tablespoon dried self-heal leaf and flower
- 1 tablespoon dried linden leaf and flower
- 1 quart boiling water
- 4 fluid ounces rose water

1. Make a hot infusion: In a mason jar, combine the peppermint, plantain, self-heal, and linden. Pour in the boiling water, cover, and steep for 20 minutes.
2. Move the jar to the refrigerator until it's cold.
3. Strain out 4 fluid ounces of the infusion and transfer to an 8-ounce bottle with a fine-mist sprayer top. Use the remaining infusion for compresses or a cooling drink. It will keep refrigerated for 3 days.

4. Add the rose water to the spray bottle. Cap the bottle and label it.
5. Apply copiously and frequently. Keep the spray refrigerated when not in use.

Cholesterol Management

Relevant tissue states: heat (inflammation)
Relevant herbal actions: anti-inflammatory, antioxidant, hepatic, hypotensive

Herbal Allies:

- Cinnamon bark
- Garlic
- Ginger
- Kelp
- Linden leaf and flower
- Rose
- Yarrow leaf and flower

High cholesterol is a *symptom*, not a freestanding problem. It is an indicator that systemic inflammation is damaging the blood vessels. Many things can cause this—blood sugar dysregulation, insufficient sleep, and stress are major factors—but the biggest one is diet.
Herbal approaches to reducing cholesterol levels primarily rely on the antioxidant power of the plants to reduce inflammation and neutralize free radicals. Eating lots of colorful fruits and vegetables, especially berries, is also very helpful.

Garlic is one of the most well-known and extensively studied herbs for reducing inflammation in the blood vessels. Adding it to your food is a simple and effective way to lower cholesterol levels and improve other blood parameters—beneficial effects start to manifest with amounts as low as two garlic cloves per day.

Antioxidant Tea

Makes about 2 cups dried herb mix (enough for 12 to 16 quarts of tea)
Gentle linden helps soften and direct the other herbs in this blend, focusing their effects on the blood vessels to improve integrity and reduce inflammation. Drink a quart or more of this tea every day.

- 1 cup dried linden leaf and flower

- ½ cup dried rose petals, hips, or a combination
- ¼ cup dried cinnamon bark
- ¼ cup dried yarrow leaf and flower
- 1 tablespoon dried ginger

1. In a medium bowl, mix all the herbs. Store in an airtight container.
2. Make a hot infusion: Prepare a kettle of boiling water. Measure 2 to 3 tablespoons of herbs per quart of water and place in a mason jar or French press. Pour in the boiling water, cover, and steep for 20 minutes or until cool enough to drink.
3.

Rose Hip Quick Jam

Makes about 3 ounces (2 servings)
This simple, tasty treat is a powerhouse of vitamin C, bioflavonoids, and antioxidant goodness. Mix this into your oatmeal or other hot cereal, spread it on toast, or just eat it by the spoonful!

- 2 tablespoons dried rosehips
- 2 fluid ounces water
- 1 teaspoon honey
- 1 teaspoon powdered cinnamon

1. In a cup or small bowl, stir together the rosehips and water. Let sit for about 1 hour, so the rosehips soften and absorb the water. They'll gel into a jam-like substance.
2. Stir in the honey and cinnamon.
3. Prepare fresh each day for maximum potency.

Cold and Flu

Relevant tissue states: heat (inflammatory immune response)
Relevant herbal actions: antiviral, immune stimulant

Herbal Allies:

- Elder
- Garlic
- Pine
- Thyme leaf
- Yarrow leaf and flower

Antibiotic treatments don't affect viral respiratory troubles like colds and flu—they only work on bacteria. Herbs, on the other hand, offer effective assistance by supporting the body's innate healing mechanisms.

Colds and flu generally cause very similar symptoms in everyone, but one or another symptom will be most acute for each person.

Elderberry Syrup

It makes about 1 quart (20 to 60 doses)

Elderberries have an amazing specific capacity to prevent flu viruses from invading the body and replicating themselves; they also fight colds and other viruses. Take this syrup in addition to remedies for your specific symptoms—1 to 3 tablespoons 3 to 5 times per day, whenever you suspect a cold or flu is present.

- 3 cups fresh elderberries
- 6 cups water
- 1 cinnamon stick or 1 teaspoon powdered cinnamon
- 1 teaspoon powdered ginger
- 1 teaspoon fennel seed
- 1 teaspoon dried chamomile flower
- 2 cups honey, plus more as needed (see Tip)

1. In a medium pot over high heat, combine the berries, water, and herbs. Bring to a boil. Reduce the heat and simmer, *uncovered*, for 1 to 2 hours or until reduced by half.
2. Use a spoon to mash the berries in the pot. Stir, simmer for 15 minutes more, and strain through a wire mesh sieve or cheesecloth. Squeeze the leftover berries well to get out every last bit of fluid. You should have between 2 and 3 cups of elderberry decoction.
3. Return the elderberry decoction to the pan and place it over low heat. Add an equal amount of honey, warming it gently as you stir to mix thoroughly with the elderberry decoction.
4. Bottle and label the syrup. It will stay in the refrigerator for several months.

TIP: Some recipes use sugar, as this creates a shelf-stable product. We try to avoid sugar, so we use honey and keep ours refrigerated. Another alternative is to add 2 cups of tincture (in addition to the decoction and honey) to your syrup—the alcohol content will preserve it. Tinctures of ginger, garlic, pine, yarrow, and thyme are all good options.

Constipation

Relevant tissue states: cold (stagnation), dryness, tension
Relevant herbal actions: bitter, carminative, demulcent, hepatic, laxative

Herbal Allies:

- Angelica
- Dandelion root
- Ginger
- Marshmallow
- Milk thistle seed
- St. John's wort leaf and flower

Sometimes, constipation is simply a sign of dehydration—drink some water! If it's a chronic issue, it may be an indication of a food allergy or simply a sign that you're not getting sufficient fiber in your diet. A good, thick, cold infusion of marshmallow solves both problems: It rehydrates better than water alone, and it includes a lot of polysaccharides and fibers that help move stool along.

Constipation, especially when ongoing, can be traced back to sluggish liver function. Bile produced by the liver is a digestive fluid, but it also lubricates the intestines; when production is low, things can get stuck. Bitters and carminatives help spur digestive function, and liver-restorative herbs (hepatics) such as milk thistle can reestablish normal function.

Bowel-Hydrating Infusion

Makes 2½ cups dried herb mix (enough for 14 to 18 quarts of tea)
A bit tastier than solo marshmallow, this is a great solution for the type of constipation that often afflicts people with dry constitutions. If you have hard-to-pass, dry, little "rabbit pellet" bowel movements, this is for you. Drink a quart or more every day.

- 1 cup dried linden leaf and flower
- 1 cup dried marshmallow root

- ¼ cup dried cinnamon bark
- ¼ cup dried licorice root

1. In a medium bowl, mix all the herbs. Store in an airtight container.
2. Make a cold infusion: Measure 2 to 4 tablespoons of herbs per quart of water and place in a mason jar or French press. Pour in cold or room-temperature water and steep for 4 to 8 hours before straining.

Bowel-Motivating Tincture

Makes 4 fluid ounces (30 to 60 doses)

These bitters and carminatives will spur the bowels to movement by stimulating bile flow and intestinal peristalsis.

- 1½ fluid ounces tincture of dandelion root
- 1½ fluid ounces tincture of St. John's wort
- ½ fluid ounce tincture of angelica root
- ½ fluid ounce tincture of ginger

1. In a small bottle, combine the tinctures. Cap the bottle and label it.
2. Take 2 to

Stings

It has happened to everyone to be stung by a mosquito, a bee, a wasp, or a jellyfish. These stings or bites cause a local inflammation of the skin with itching, redness, and swelling. An over-scratched sting can become infected from time to time or in the worst cases can lead to anaphylactic shock due to an allergy reaction. For this reason, it is important not to underestimate them and call for help in case you advise any sign of air duct closure.

Symptomatology:

- Redness
- Inflammation
- Pain

Actions Required:

- Antibacterial
- Anti-inflammatory

Recommended Herbs:

- Echinacea root
- Peppermint leaves
- Witch Hazel leaves
- Heal-all leaves and flowers
- Yarrow leaves
- Agrimony flower
- Marigold flower

Soothing Compress

- 1 pint of water
- 8 oz. Peppermint Dried Leaves
- 4 oz. Epsom Salt

Directions:
Bring the water to a boil. Reduce the heat, add the peppermint leaves and let simmer for 10 minutes. Let it cool for five to ten minutes. Take a towel and pour some of the decoction on it. It must be wet but not dripping.
Place the wet towel in the sore zone for 20 minutes.

Tincture for Stings

- ¼ oz. Apple Cider Vinegar
- 1 tsp Heal-all Tincture
- 1 tsp Yarrow Tincture
- 1 tsp Rose Tincture
- 1 tsp Witch Hazel Water Tincture

Directions:
Combine all the ingredients in an amber glass bottle. Apply topically.

Wash for Stings

- 1tsp Echinacea root (powder)
- 1tsp Heal-all
- 1tbsp Yarrow Dried Leaves
- 1 cup distilled water, boiling

Directions:
Combine the ingredients in a glass or plastic container. Let rest for 1-2 hours, strain, and wash the sore part with it.

Ointment for Stings

- ¼ lb. Coconut oil
- 1 tsp dried marigold
- 1 tsp dried agrimony

Directions:

Melt the coconut oil in a water bath. Add the herbs, stir and let on low heat for two hours. Strain and pour in a mason jar, let it cool down, and then close the lid.

Apply on the sore part whenever it is needed.

Strains and Sprains

Sprains happen when a ligament or a tendon is damaged following an unnatural movement of the articulation. Strains are instead muscular fiber tearing or over elongation due to unnatural movement of the joint.

The two injuries frequently happen simultaneously and cause pain during the movement, severe limitations to the mobility of the affected limb, inflammation, swelling, and bruises.

It is important not to underestimate sprains in particular, because they can become chronic and permanently affect the mobility of the articulation. Once the joint is healed, it is also important to strengthen the articulation's muscle to avoid the injury from happening again.

Symptomatology:

- Inflammation

Actions Required:

- Anti-inflammation
- Circulatory stimulant

Recommended Herbs:

- Ginger root
- Solomon's seal root
- St. John's Wort root
- Heal-all leaves and flowers
- Meadowsweet leaves and flowers
- Cinnamon bark
- Peppermint leaves
- Lizard Tail root
- Wintergreen leaves
- Black Cohosh root
- Ashwagandha root

- Raspberry root
- White Willow bark

Analgesic Tea 1

- 1 tsp Raspberry root
- 1 tsp Willow bark
- 1 cup distilled boiling water

Directions:
Pour boiling water over the herbs mixture. Let rest for half an hour—strain and drink throughout the day.

Analgesic Tea 2

- 1 tsp Ashwagandha root
- 1 tsp Black Cohosh root
- 1 cup distilled boiling water

Directions:
Pour boiling water over the herbs mixture. Let rest minutes before straining. Drink one cup throughout the day.

Analgesic Ointment

- 2 tbsp. Wintergreen leaves tincture
- 3 tbsp. Lizard Tail root tincture
- 1 lb. Coconut Oil

Directions:
Melt the coconut oil in a water bath. Add the herbs, stir and let on low heat for two hours. Strain and pour in a mason jar, let it cool down, and then close the lid.
Apply on the sore part whenever needed and massage.

Sprain Healing Ointment

- 1 tbsp. Ashwagandha root oil
- 1 tbsp. St. John's Wort root oil
- 1 tbsp. Solomon's seal root oil
- 1 tbsp. Heal-all leaves and flowers oil
- 1 tbsp. Meadowsweet root oil

Directions:
Combine the essential oils in the proportion indicated above. Place 10 drops on your hands, rub vigorously to warm up the oil, and massage the sore part.

Teeth and Mouth Ailments

In this chapter, we will treat Gingivitis, Abscesses, and Canker sores. **Gingivitis** is an inflammation of the gum tissue. It manifests as reddening, swelling, and at times bleeding of the gums. The cause of Gingivitis is the accumulation of plaque on teeth and its removal will almost certainly reverse the disease. If untreated, gingivitis can lead to gingival shrinkage and loose teeth.

An **Abscess** is a different kettle of fish. It is a more severe condition related to a serious bacterial infection, which causes the production of pus. Abscesses can appear anywhere in the body: folliculitis, whitlows, and mouth abscesses are the most common forms.

They manifest as swelling, heat, and a reddening of the part (like pimples) and are often accompanied by fever.

Antibiotics are the common medical treatment for them but, as you will probably know, they are like an insecticide: they destroy everything in their path, from the germs that cause the infection to the intestinal bacterial flora (that is essential to our digestion), the white blood cells (who fight the infections), and the lymphocytes (who produce the antibodies).

Herbs could help you effectively fight infections and inflammation without these side effects from this point of view.

Finally, **Canker Sores** are small sores that can appear on lips, tongue, and throat. They present as white or yellow ulcers surrounded by inflamed tissue.

The causes of canker sores may be a viral infection, poor dental hygiene, or lack of vitamins and nutrients.

Symptomatology:

- Inflammation and laxity of the tissue

Actions Required:

- Anti-inflammatory
- Antibacterial

- Astringent

Recommended Herbs:

- Uva Ursi leaves
- Yarrow leaves
- Plantain leaves
- Heal-all leaves and flowers
- calendula flowers
- Licorice root
- Barberry fruit and leaves
- White Oak bark and leaves
- Echinacea root
- Oregon grape root
- Lizard Tail Root
- Sage leaves
- Thyme leaves
- Goldenrod leaves and flowers
- Chamomile

Anti-Inflammatory Mouthwash

Ingredients:

- 8 oz. Distilled water
- 2 tsp. Epsom Salt
- 2 oz. Uva Ursi tincture
- 2 oz. Yarrow tincture
- 1 oz. Plantain tincture
- 1 oz. Heal-all tincture
- 1 oz. Calendula tincture
- ½ oz. Heal-all tincture
- ½ oz. Licorice tincture

Directions:

Combine all the ingredients above in a glass container.

After brushing your teeth, take a mouthful of the mouthwash and swish for about 4 minutes.

Anti-Abscess Mouthwash

Ingredients:

- 20 oz. Distilled boiling water
- 4tbsp. Barberries
- 4 tbsp. Oak bark
- 4 tsp Echinacea root
- 4 tsp Oregon grape root powdered

Directions:

Combine all the ingredients above in a glass container. Let it rest 6 hours before straining.

After brushing your teeth, take a mouthful of the mouthwash and swish for about 4 minutes.

Anti-Abscess Tea

Ingredients:

- ¼ oz. Echinacea Tincture
- ½ oz. Lizard Tail root Tincture
- 25oz distilled water

Directions:

Heat the water and put the tinctures in it. Makes 5 cups to drink throughout the day.

Note:

Particularly effective on skin abscesses

Mouthwash for Canker Sores

Ingredients:

- 4 tbsp. Barberry tea
- 4 tbsp. Echinacea
- 4 tbsp. White oak tea
- 4 tbsp. Oregon grape root tea

Directions:

Combine all the ingredients above in a glass container.

After brushing your teeth, take a mouthful of the mouthwash and swish for about 4 minutes.

Conclusion

In this third book, we have described the herbal medical preparations used by Native Americans to soothe and effectively treat the most common ailments. All the remedies have been designed to be made in the comfort of your kitchen, with herbs, you can buy in your herbal shop.

This book will be helpful to the reader if they are interested in these herbal remedies because it describes each remedy with a detailed description of what it does and why it is effective. Each author had their specific reason to write this book; however, they all wanted to bring good health for people. The author's specific reasons are as follows:

1) To guide readers on how to make herbal remedies.
2) To show how these herbal remedies can help fight infections and diseases.
3) Introduce a new way for readers to deal with their health problems.
4) Inform readers about different herbs that can help heal injuries and illnesses.
5) Provide detailed information about herbs that the reader may not be familiar with.
6) Show the readers how they can use their kitchen ingredients to create herbal remedies for them to use in case of an emergency.

I sincerely hope that this will be just the beginning of your journey and that you will increase your knowledge on Native American medicine for a healthier and better way to treat the common disease without relying on industrial drugs and medication.

If you have enjoyed this book, feel free to leave a review to share your experience.

My best wishes and may the Spirit guide your journey!

BOOK 4

Natural American Native Herbal Recipes

Introduction

Herbalism is the study of how plants and herbs can be used for medicinal purposes.

Throughout human history, people have invested their efforts to find the medicinal properties of plants. Whether it's through experimentation or trial and error, people will always look to nature for cures.

Herbalism is based on the belief that plants have healing properties that can help treat sickness and disease.

The use of herbs dates back to ancient times.

One of the earliest recorded cures was garlic juice applied to a wound to stop bleeding around 1550 B.C.(1).

Native Americans cultivated herbs because they knew they had healing properties.

They also knew how to make these herbs grow and mature, which helped them create remedies that would last longer.

What makes native American herbalism different?

Unlike the use of "modern" pharmaceuticals, traditional herbalism aims to target the root cause of any ailment and cures it naturally.

Native Americans used this approach to treat illnesses, pain, and physical disorders.

There are a lot of great benefits to using these herbs for your health! You don't need to take expensive medications or have an appointment with a doctor; all you have to do is make herbal remedies and watch your problems disappear. Plus, these remedies are free and easy to make for yourself!

There are many natural ways to improve your health, from using DIY recipes made at home that are all-natural or going on a cleanse to detoxify your body. This will help clear your mind and help you make more sense of the world around you.

This eBook will show you how to use herbs in your life, and how to be naturally healthy without spending a lot of money on expensive prescriptions. These DIY herbal recipes will help you live a better life, easily and affordably!

In this book, I would like to talk about one of my favorite subjects: herbal remedies. I have been using these for many years and trust in

them 100%. Try these recipes; I am sure you will be pleased with the results!
What are you waiting for?
Go ahead and start improving your life with these natural herbal recipes today!

Most Common DIY Herbal Recipes

Herbal Tea Recipes

Herbal teas differ widely from one another and the general teas because they do not come from the same plant. They are the combinations of flowers, herbs, and dried fruits, which are brewed like tea. Herbal teas contain no caffeine, often lower blood pressure, have delicious flavors, and improve digestion. They also often contain no calories and no sugar.

Raspberry Tea

Serving size: make one serving
Brewing time: 10 minutes

Ingredients:

- One c. water
- ¼ c. dried raspberry leaves
- ¼ c. dried lemon grass
- ½ c. dried chamomile flowers
- ½ c. dried orange peel

Directions:

1. Mix all the dried herbs listed above.
2. Boil water.
3. Add 1 tsp. of tea mixture in a cup.
4. Pour hot water over it. Cover and steep for 5-10 minutes. The longer the time, the more tannin is extracted.
5. Consume hot, cold, or iced.

Nutrition facts per serving: Calories: 40Carbs: 12 g Fat: 0 g Protein 0 g Sodium: 2 mg Sugar: 0 g

Hibiscus- Ginger Tea

Serving size: make 4 cups
Brewing time: 15 minutes

Ingredients:

- 4 c. water
- 1 tbsp. hibiscus leaves
- 1 tbsp. grated fresh ginger
- 3-5 mint leaves

Directions:

1. Boil water in a pot.
2. Take hibiscus and ginger and blend in another pot.
3. Pour hot water over the tea mixture, cover and steep for 10-12 minutes.
4. The color of the tea will turn ruby red, then add mint leaves for fresh flavor.
5. Serve hot or cold.

Nutrition facts per serving: *Calories: 1 Carbs: 1 g Fat: 0 g Protein: 0 g Sodium: 1 mg Sugar: 0 g*

Mint Tea

Serving size: make 2 servings
Brewing time: 8 minutes

Ingredients:

- 2 c. water
- 15-20 fresh mint leaves
- 2 lemon slices
- 1 tsp. honey (optional)

Directions:

1. In a teapot, boil the water.
2. Remove from the heat and add in all the mint leaves. Cover the pot and steep for 5 minutes. Increase the time for a strong flavor of mint.
3. Pour in a cup or glass.
4. Add honey and garnish with a lemon slice.
5. Enjoy hot or iced.

Nutrition facts per serving: *Calories: 150 Carbs: 26 g Fat: 5 g Protein: 3 g Sodium: 75 mg Sugar: 15 g*

Sweet and Spicy Herb Tea

Serving size: makes 1 serving
Brewing time: 10 minutes

Ingredients:

- 1 c. water
- ½ tbsp. cloves
- 1 tbsp. dried stevia
- ¼ c. cinnamon stick
- ¼ c. dried orange zest
- ¼ c. dried chamomile flowers
- ½ c. dried lemon verbena

Directions:

1. Make the blend and use 1 tsp. tea mixture.
2. Boil the water and pour it over the tea mixture.
3. Cover the pot and let it steep for 5 minutes or more.
4. Strain into a cup and serve hot. Alternatively, pour over ice in the glass and serve cold.
5. Enjoy the sweet and spicy taste.

Nutrition facts per serving: *Calories: 110 Carbs: 31 g Fat: 3 g Protein: 2 g Sodium: 16 mg Sugar: 1 g*

Basil Tea

Serving size: makes 1 serving
Brewing time: 5 minutes

Ingredients:

- 1 c. water
- 1 tsp. basil leaves
- ¼ tsp. dried ginger
- ½ tsp. cinnamon powder
- 1 tsp honey (optional)

Directions:

1. Boil the water and add the basil leaves, ginger and cinnamon.
2. Steep it for 5 minutes.
3. Strain and add honey to improve the taste.
4. Pour in a cup and serve hot.

Nutrition facts per serving: *Calories: 10 Carbs: 3 g Fat: 0 g Protein: 0 g Sodium: 1 mg Sugar: 0 g*

Decoctions are another form of herbal remedies. This is the extraction of medicinal qualities from the herb by steeping it in water until the water gets its color, smell and taste traits. Decoctions are made through the process, allowing plant material or herbal substances to release their active ingredients during boiling. In this way, various natural chemical components present inside the herb can be easily released by mixing it with warm water. Decoctions are widely used sources of herbal medicine in herbalism. When roots or barks of plants contain medicinal benefits, it is hard to obtain extracts from these hard parts of plants, such as willow bark. Decoctions are used to extract tannins, which are harsh and bitter and help in digestion.

Decoctions have been used to treat many different health problems over centuries, especially in herbal medicine. The process is also very useful for treating several health disorders, including blood purification, liniments for skin problems such as acne and dermatitis, tonics for dryness, and irritations such as eczema psoriasis.

Often they are known to be useful for treating musculoskeletal problems such as rheumatism, arthritis, cramps etc.

Making Herb-Infused Decoctions

Herbs can be used to make herbal decoctions but they can also be used to prepare infusions. This is the process of preparing herbs by boiling the leaves with water, usually for a longer time than what is needed to make decoctions. In this way the active ingredients would be more effective because they concentrate inside the water and not simple in the herbs themselves. Decoctions are made through boiling herbs in water until the water gets its color, smell and taste traits. In this way, various natural chemical components present inside the plant can be easily released by mixing it with warm water. Decoctions are widely used sources of herbal medicine in herbalism. However, they can also be made from bark or roots or barks that do not contain as many medicinal benefits as extracts from leaves, flowers, seeds, etc.

Here is a list of Decoctions for you to tryout;

Basil Decoction

Method:

Boil 2 – 3 tbsp of Basil leaves in a cup of water.
Cover with a lid and steep for 10-15 minutes.

If you want the mixture to be more concentrated, you can increase the amount of Basil leaves you to use when preparing your decoction.
Take your hot decoction and strain it using a strainer or cheese cloth into an empty cup.

Thoroughly clean up the filter if used before storing it for later use.
Drink this hot herbal tea twice daily for best results.
Other ingredients that you may want to include in your decoction are mint leaves, rosemary or lavender.
Also note that Rosemary can be used instead of Basil for a more robust decoction.

German Chamomile Decoction

Method:

Boil 1 – 2 tbsp of Chamomile flowers in a cup of water.
Cover with a lid and steep for 10-15 minutes.
Take your Hot Chamomile decoction and strain it using a strainer or cheesecloth into an empty cup.
Thoroughly clean up the filter if used before storing it for later use.
Drink this hot herbal tea twice daily for best results.
You may want to include other ingredients in your decoction: mint leaves, rosemary or lavender.
Also note that Rosemary can be used instead of Chamomile for a more robust decoction.

Chicory Decoction

Method:

Boil 1 – 2 tbsp of Chicory roots in a cup of water.

Cover with a lid and steep for 5-10 minutes.

Take your hot decoction and strain it using a strainer or cheesecloth into an empty cup.

Thoroughly clean up the filter if used before storing it for later use.

Drink this hot herbal tea twice daily for best results.

You may want to include other ingredients in your decoction: mint leaves, rosemary or lavender.

Chicory can be used instead of Chamomile for a more robust decoction.

Ginger Decoction

Method:

Boil 1 – 2 tbsp of Ginger in a cup of water.

Cover with a lid and steep for 10-15 minutes.

Take your hot decoction and strain it using a strainer or cheesecloth into an empty cup.

Thoroughly clean up the filter if used before storing it for later use.

Drink this hot herbal tea twice daily for best results.

Other ingredients that you may want to include in your decoction are mint leaves, rosemary or lavender.

Ginkgo berry Decoction

Method:

Boil 1 – 2 tbsp of Ginkgo in a cup of water.

Cover with a lid and steep for 10-15 minutes.

Take your hot decoction and strain it using a strainer or cheesecloth into an empty cup.

Thoroughly clean up the filter if used before storing it for later use.

Drink this hot herbal tea twice daily for best results.

You may want to include other ingredients in your decoction: mint leaves, rosemary or lavender.

Ginseng Decoction

Method:

Boil 1 – 2 tbsp of Ginseng in a cup of water.

Cover with a lid and steep for 10-15 minutes.

Take your hot decoction and strain it using a strainer or cheesecloth into an empty cup.

Thoroughly clean up the filter if used before storing it for later use.

Drink this hot herbal tea twice daily for best results.

Other ingredients that you may want to include in your decoction are mint leaves, rosemary or lavender.

Horsetail Decoction

Method:

Boil 1 – 2 tbsp of Horsetail in a cup of water.

Cover with a lid and steep for 10-15 minutes.

Take your hot decoction and strain it using a strainer or cheesecloth into an empty cup.

Thoroughly clean up the filter if used before storing it for later use.

Drink this hot herbal tea twice daily for best results.

You may want to include other ingredients in your decoction: mint leaves, rosemary or lavender.

Irish Moss Decoction

Method:

Boil 1 – 2 tbsp of Irish moss in a cup of water.

Cover with a lid and steep for 10-15 minutes.

Take your hot decoction and strain it using a strainer or cheesecloth into an empty cup.

Thoroughly clean up the filter if used before storing it for later use.
Drink this hot herbal tea twice daily for best results.
Other ingredients that you may want to include in your decoction are mint leaves, rosemary, or lavender.

Popsicles can be made from various sources, such as fruit juice, herbs, fruits, and vegetables. Popsicles are mainly made from fresh ingredients to provide health benefits with no preservatives or artificial flavorings.

Popsicles can be made using fresh herbs as an ingredient in the mixture of the frozen solid state of water. Herb-infused popsicle recipes can be found online. Herb-infused popsicles usually have different flavors like mint or orange. Some other popular flavors include pineapple and strawberry, which is a combination of both lemon and orange.

The use of herbs on popsicles can provide some great benefits. Herbs are known to have antioxidant, anti-inflammatory, antibacterial, antiviral, and analgesic effects. A mixture of herbs can provide a unique taste to your popsicles.

Ginger and mint popsicles are among the most common herb popsicles sold in grocery stores because of their refreshing taste and health benefits. Ginger is known to have properties with anti-inflammatory effects and improve digestive problems. Mint has antioxidant properties which help protect the cells from damage by free radicals. Mint also has antibacterial and anti-inflammatory properties.

Making Herb-Infused Popsicles

Herbs can be used not only to flavor our foods but also can be used in herbal medicine. Herbal medicine is a form of complementary treatment that employs herbs in combination with other drugs. In most cases, it is a form of alternative medicine that relies on the healing power of plants rather than modern medication or surgery. In this kind of therapy, modern medicine and herbs are combined to help patients improve their health and regain their wholeness from illness. Herbal medicine is also used to give the body a boost of energy and rejuvenation.

The medicinal herbs can be infused in popsicles. Preserves and herbs are used because they combine well with popsicle ingredients.

Popsicle molds can be purchased or are homemade from old molds that you can buy at craft stores. Popsicle sticks, parchment paper, and sticks can also be purchased at craft stores. Food coloring can also be added to create different colors of popsicles.

Ginger Mint Popsicles

1 cup of coconut water or any fruit juice of your choice (if you are on a low-calorie diet, you can replace it with water)
2-inch ginger root, peeled, sliced into 1/4 pieces
4 to 6 fresh mint leaves
Process: Add freshly sliced ginger and mint leaves to the blender. Pour in the fruit juice or coconut water. Blend until smooth. Pour into popsicle molds and freeze overnight.

Cucumber and Herb Popsicles

1 cup of fruit juice or coconut water
2 cucumbers, peeled, sliced into 1/4 pieces
3-5 fresh mint leaves
Process: Place the jars in the blender. Add in mint leaves and make sure that they are completely blended. Pour in fruit juice or coconut water. Blend until smooth. Pour into popsicle molds and freeze overnight.

Fruit and Herb Popsicles

1 cup of fruit juice or coconut water
2-inch piece of fresh ginger, peeled, sliced into 1/4 pieces
5 to 6 fresh mint leaves
Process: Place the jars in the blender. Add in mint leaves and ginger. Make sure that all the pieces are completely blended. Pour in fruit juice or coconut water. Blend until smooth. Pour into popsicle molds and freeze overnight.

Herbal Popsicles

1 cup of fruit juice or coconut water

5 to 7 fresh mint leaves

Process: Place the jars in the blender. Add mint leaves and make sure that they are completely blended. Pour in fruit juice or coconut water. Blend until smooth. Pour into popsicle molds and freeze overnight.

Cucumber and Mint Popsicles

1 cup of fruit juice or coconut water

1–2-inch piece of fresh ginger, peeled

5 to 7 mint leaves

Process: Place the jars in the blender. Add ginger and mint. Make sure that they are completely blended. Pour in fruit juice or coconut water. Blend until smooth. Pour into popsicle molds and freeze overnight.

Ice cubes

Ice cubes are a fantastic source of herbal delivery, especially when compared to tea or tinctures, which are the most common forms of herbal delivery. Ice cubes are flavored with herbs; thus, the flavor of the herbs will be easily absorbed by the body once it is melted inside.

Ice cubes can be created in various ways such as herb-infused waters and sauces.

Herb-infused ice cubes may also be a nice gift idea for friends and family during celebrations and special occasions.

Liquid herbal medicine can be frozen after boiling and rapid cooling, a process called thawing. Alternatively, an herbal decoction can be used to make ice cubes.

Baths

The body's largest organ is the skin, which has a very complicated structure and very diverse in properties and colors. The skin is a crucial component in the body's immune system, as it provides a physical barrier from the outside. Some special layers of the skin contain various chemicals to protect us from diseases, worms, and microbes.

Bath treatment with herbs can be a great way to deal with the chills and make you feel very relaxed after a hard day's work. Using herbal baths can help you achieve healthy skin and helps maintain overall body health.

Herbs that can be used for baths are either made into decoctions, capsules, or tinctures.

Hot baths are essential because they can help dissolve the herbs and increase their effectiveness, thus improving the quality of the bath. It is important to avoid extreme hot baths because they raise body temperature and can cause hyperthermia.

The decoction can be used for baths as they are delicious and have skin-nourishing properties.

The most popular herbs for baths are mint and lemon balm. Mint extracts are used not only for baths, but also for aromatherapy. Lemon balm can be used to relieve stress and improve blood circulation.

Here is a list of herbal baths that can help you achieve healthy skin:

Lavender Bath

Preparation:

Add 1 to 2 cups of dried lavender flower to your bathtub.

Boil a pot of water and add 1/2 cup of Epsom salt.

Pour the mixture into the bathtub and then get into the tub after you've added water.

Soak for 5 to 10 minutes.

Use caution because the Epsom salt may irritate those who are sensitive to it.

Sage Bath

Preparation:

Place 1/4 cup of dried sage in your bathtub and add hot water.

Steep for 5 to 10 minutes before getting into the tub.

For extra effect, you can leave the herbs in the tub after your bath.

It is recommended not to use this herbal treatment if you are pregnant or breastfeeding because sage has some properties that can make you feel like you're on an intense trip.

Rose Petal Bath

Place 8 to 10 organic rose petals into your bathtub.

Rose petals are an excellent source of vitamin C, which helps brighten and soften skin.

Steep the rose petals in hot water for 3 to 5 minutes before getting into the tub.

Rose glyceride is a substance found in rose petals that can soothe irritations and inflammation caused by eczema and acne.

Ginger Bath

Ginger is an essential element to improving your skin's health.

The best ginger is fresh ginger, and it can be added to your bath either as a decoction or powder.

If you make the decoction, be sure to use two parts water for one part ginger root.

Add 1/2 cup of Epsom salt and 1 cup of fresh ginger root for each person taking a bath.

Use 3 to 4 cups of hot water for each person taking a bath.

Steep in a pot for 5-10 minutes.

When ready to take a bath, use 1/2 cup of the mixture with the Epsom salt and add it to your bathwater.

Soak for 5 to 10 minutes before rinsing off with fresh water.

Precautions: do not use this herbal treatment if you have high blood pressure because ginger can increase blood pressure levels. Also, do not take this herbal bath if you are pregnant.

Infants can also use herbal medicine if their mums have been using herbs. Breast milk contains many herbs, which are essential for the well-being of infants. Infants can be given herbal teas or capsules to help clear symptoms of colds and flu and reduce allergic reactions.

A mother and her child both can benefit from the positive effects of natural herbs. They both can avoid using pharmaceutical drugs and chemicals to treat conditions that are often caused by stress, diet, pollutants, or aging.

Another significant benefit is to insert potent herbal antibacterial medicine inside an infant to make him/her more immune to side effects of getting sick from antibacterial is to introduce them from the mother's breast milk. It will boost the natural immunization responses in both mother and her infant. Common herbs commonly used in the skin and associated with breast milk are alel5, oil of citronella, essential oils including lemon, lavender and other herbs.

The advantages of using herbal infant teas made by mothers are that they are just made using natural extracts from plants. In addition to herbal infant teas made by mothers, infant teas can be easily purchased from health food stores or online at websites such as eternahealth.com.

In terms of safety, herbal infant teas are safe for both mother and the baby as long as they are made using natural and non-toxic ingredients.

Herbal infant teas can interact with other herbs or medications used by the mother. Therefore, mothers must take herbs without interactions with other medicines, while breastfeeding at the same time.

Here is a list of breast milk herbal that can be beneficial to infants:

Lemon Balm

Lemon balm has been found to help infants with colic, fussiness, and other digestive problems. Lemon balm has also been known to soothe infant fussiness and relieve cramps. Studies have shown that lemon balm can help stimulate breast milk secretion and increase the number of nutrients in the milk of nursing mothers who take them.

Method:

Add 1/4 teaspoon of finely ground lemon balm powder or 2 to 3 drops of lemon balm essential oil to 4 ounces of breastmilk.

Warm the breast milk either by the microwave or on the stove.

Serve your baby.

Repeat every two hours during the day and as needed for relief.

Do not use this herbal treatment if the mother is breastfeeding a preterm infant.

Chamomile

Chamomile is one of the most common herbs used in treating children suffering from colic, fever, and teething. Chamomile is also known to help reduce swelling, soothe irritable newborns, and soothe fevers. Chamomile can also be used for making herbal infant teas or tinctures.

Method:

Add 1/4 teaspoon of finely ground chamomile or 2 to 3 drops of chamomile essential oil to 4 ounces of breastmilk.

Warm the breast milk either by the microwave or on the stove.

Serve your baby.

Repeat every two hours during the day and as needed for relief.

Do not use this herbal treatment if the mother is breastfeeding a preterm infant.

Calendula

Calendula is also known as marigold. Calendula can be used to make herbal teas for infants, or they can also be added to a bath in a little bit of water. Calendula has strong anti-inflammatory properties.

Method:

Add 1/4 teaspoon of finely ground calendula or 2 to 3 drops of calendula essential oil to 4 ounces of breastmilk.

Warm the breast milk either by the microwave or on the stove.

Serve your baby.

Repeat every two hours during the day and as needed for relief.

Do not use this herbal treatment if the mother is breastfeeding a preterm infant.

Washcloths

Washcloths are used to gently clean the baby's face, lips, eyes and genitals. They can be used in the bath area as well. They can be used on a critically ill patient who cannot survive an active bath. In this comfortable way, medicine can easily be applied to the skin, and thus it can be transferred to a deeper area of the body through diffusion. Washcloths can be warm by using hot infusions of medicine when specific heating impacts are needed, or they can be cold when benefits of cold are needed. It all depends upon personal choice as well as symptoms of illnesses. For acute injuries, for example, brushing and combat sports fights, cold washcloths with specific benefits of ice and anti-inflammatory medicine can be a smart choice to limit swelling and bruising and impede bleeding from fresh wounds. Cold also has anesthetic properties, which make it a natural painkiller.

When used warm, washcloths can stimulate blood flow due to vasodilatory effects as well as a soothing response of the body can also be obtained. Herbal washcloths can be applied to the area of an injury.

Here are different ways to make herbal washcloths to be used for different conditions:

Eye wash

Preparation:

Add a few drops of water into the eye spray bottle.

Fill the rest of the bottle with peppermint essential oil.

Use these eyedrops to clean the eye area.

This is very good for people who suffer from dry eyes, as they can treat them with one quick and simple treatment. Refrigerate in an airtight container after each use to ensure potency.

Eye wash can also be used for other purposes, such as treating conjunctivitis, blepharitis, and other eye issues.

Tongue wash

Preparation:

Add a few drops of water to the tongue spray bottle.

Fill the rest of the bottle with Thyme essential oil.

Use this tongue spray to clean the area around the mouth and in its presence; you would feel a soothing sensation on your tongue.

This is a very good treatment if your mouth is filled with bad breath and a cleansing of the inside of your mouth. It can be stored for two weeks in an airtight container after use.

Tongue wash can be used on other parts of the body such as the inner thigh area, groin area, armpit, and any other areas that may need a light cleaning and soothing.

Armpit wash

Preparation:

Add a few drops of water to the armpit spray bottle.

Fill the rest of the bottle with Lavender essential oil.

Use this armpit spray to clean your armpits and you will feel a soothing sensation on your skin.

This is very good for people who work in the construction field, as it will help remove odors from the body and develop an anti-bacterial treatment for skin infections. It can be stored for two weeks in an airtight container after use.

The armpit wash can also be used on other areas of the body such as the groin area, inner thigh area, and back of the neck to get a good cleaning.

Inner thigh wash

Preparation:

Add a few drops of water to the inner thigh spray bottle.

Fill the rest of the bottle with Lavender essential oil.

Use this inner thigh spray to clean the area around your groin and it will make you feel a soothing sensation.

This is very good for people who play sports, as it will help remove sweat and bacteria that may cause infections. It can create an anti-bacterial treatment for skin infections. It can be stored for two weeks in an airtight container after use.

The inner thigh wash can be used on other areas such as the armpit, groin, inner wrist, and any other not-to-be-replaced areas.

Inner wrist wash

Preparation:

Add a few drops of water to the inner wrist spray bottle.

Fill the rest of the bottle with Lavender essential oil.

Use this inner wrist spray to clean the area around your hand, making you feel a soothing sensation.

This is very good for people who work in the construction field, as it will help remove odors from the body and develop an anti-bacterial treatment for skin infections. It can be stored for two weeks in an airtight container after use.

The inner wrist wash can also be used on other areas of the body such as the groin area, armpit, inner thigh area, or any other not-to-be-replaced areas.

Compresses

Compresses are warm medicinal pastes that are formed from many potent herbs. Compresses can be used to cleanse the skin and also provide nourishment and immune support.

Compresses can be warm or cold depending on your personal choice. Compresses can be created through herbal packing, steeping plants in water, then removing the water extracts of herbs before transferring them to liquid form. It is usually done by using a blender to powder herbs into small particles, and this powder is added directly into water to create the paste.

There are also several different ways in which compresses can be processed. One way is to use a combination of herbs and other natural compounds found within the plants, such as vitamins B and C. The most common will work for most people, but research findings have shown that particular combinations of herbs can provide greater effects than others. The most common type of compress is an infusion, although packs can be made by simply adding tea bags and stewing the herbs in boiling water.

Compresses are useful for different purposes. The first purpose is to make the skin cleaner, which helps prevent infections and skin disorders by simply cleaning the dirt off it. The second purpose is to provide nourishment to the skin to heal itself from any ailments, such as bed sores or cuts. Finally, compresses also help with circulation and immune support.

Find a list of herbs below that can be used to create different compresses for various purposes.

Cleanse and Heal

Skin Cleanser

Preparation:

Stir all of the ingredients together until it completely smooths.

Place 4 inches of hot water in the pan, pour the mixture into it, and place on the stove for five minutes.

Remove the pan from heat and cover with a lid or towel for about ten minutes.

Use two to three times a day.

Treat Burns

Burn Treatment

Preparation:

Stir all of the ingredients together until it completely smooths.

Place 4 inches of hot water in the pan, pour the mixture into it, and place on the stove for five minutes.

Remove the pan from heat and cover with a lid or towel for about ten minutes.

Use two to three times a day.

Remove Infection

Breast Infection Compress

Preparation:

Stir all of the ingredients together until it completely smooths.

Place 4 inches of hot water in the pan, pour the mixture into it, and place on the stove for five minutes.

Remove the pan from heat and cover with a lid or towel for about ten minutes.

Use two to three times a day.

Boost Immunity

Immunity-Boosting Compress

Preparation:

Stir all of the ingredients together until it completely smooths.

Place 4 inches of hot water in the pan, pour the mixture into it, and place on the stove for five minutes.

Remove the pan from heat and cover with a lid or towel for about ten minutes.

Use two to three times a day.

Poultices

Poultice or Marham is a type of herbal medicine applied to skin sores and wounds directly to achieve healing at maximum pace and unlock bactericidal and anti-inflammatory benefits. Poultices work through herbal extraction, which is the process of extracting medicinal qualities from herbs by steeping them in water until the water gets its color, smell and taste traits. A poultice is applied to the skin directly with warm washcloths or warm towels.

A poultice can be made by using roots, leaves, flowers and fruits of plants. Once made, poultices can be used on the skin to lock moisture into it due to its high hydrating properties.

Herbs used for poultices include mint, thyme and chamomile.

When herbs are used as poultices, the healing of wounds is done quickly and effectively. Thus, a poultice is very useful in treating common skin infections such as boils or acne, many types of hemorrhages, cuts and scratches, and other open wounds.

Again, it is a popular form of medicine in traditional Chinese, Indian, and Muslim herbalism. It is so easy to apply the poultices that they can be applied to gums in the mouth and on the lips to treat herpes and other STDs symptoms. Any fresh, damp, or dried herbs can be used to make poultices. Another effective way to apply them is to keep them on wounds for more extended periods to achieve maximum absorption. It is a widely used method of administration in herbal dentistry because it is by far the safest method to be used in the oral cavity. A poultice can be left overnight or longer in the mouth to avoid bruising and sores in the mouth. It will also help improve the freshness of the mouth and thus promote a better odor in the breath. It is essential to know the dosage of the herb in a poultice. A poultice is a damp or less wet type of medication, more like a paste that can be made by mixing water, tea, or decoction in a dried paste of herb. A mixture of different herbs can also make a poultice to unlock many benefits hidden in these different herbs. It is a fantastic strategy that many herbalists use.

For example, an analgesic herb containing pain killer properties can be mixed with antioxidant, anti-inflammatory, or any bactericidal herb to achieve all these impacts by a single use of poultice. A great recipe involves herbal tea with blueberry and willow to unlock the actions of all these three herbs in a single poultice.

Find a list of herbs below that can be used to create different poultices for various purposes.

Thrust Healing

Upper Back Poultice

Preparation:

Add 2 cups of water to the pot, bring it to a boil.

Add the herbs and simmer for about 10 minutes.

Turn off the stove, cool for about 5 minutes.

Place the poultice on the affected area and keep it there for at least 1 hour or overnight for best results.

Unlock Antibiotic and Bactericidal Properties

Antibiotic Poultice

Preparation:

Mix one cup of willow bark with 1/4 ounce of dried blueberries.

Add one cup of water to the pot, bring it to a boil.

Add the herbs and simmer for about 10 minutes.

Turn off the stove, cool for about 5 minutes.

Place the poultice on the affected area and keep it there for at least 1 hour or overnight for best results.

Unlock Wound Healing

Cuts and Scratches Poultice

Preparation:

Add 1 cup of chamomile, 1/2 cup of thyme, 2 cups of water to the pot, bring it to a boil.

Add the herbs and simmer for about 10 minutes.

Turn off the stove, cool for about 5 minutes.

Place the poultice on the affected area and keep it there for at least 1 hour or overnight for best results.

Unlock Essence of Blueberry

Plain Poultice

Preparation:

Mix one spoonful of blueberry and one spoonful of mint.

Add one cup of water to the pot, bring it to a boil.

Add the herbs and simmer for about 10 minutes.

Turn off the stove, cool for about 5 minutes. Place the poultice on the affected area and keep it there for at least 1 hour or overnight for best results.

Unlock Essence of Mint

Pregnancy Poultice

Preparation:

Add one spoonful of mint to eight spoonsful of water.

Add one cup of chamomile, one cup of thyme, two cups of water to the pot, bring it to a boil.

Add the herbs and simmer for about 10 minutes.

Turn off the stove, cool for about 5 minutes.

Place the poultice on the affected area and keep it there for at least 1 hour or overnight for best results.

Unlock Essence Of Thyme

Herpes Poultice

Preparation:

Boil one cup of water with one spoonful of thyme and chamomile leaves in a pot.

Add hot water to the mixture until half full, remove the bottle from heat and let it cool for 10 minutes.

Stir the mixture, add a cup of white vinegar.

Place on the affected area and cover it with a towel to warm the poultice faster.

Leave the poultice on for at least 1 hour or overnight for best results.

Tinctures

Tinctures are drops of herbs in liquid form, which is usually alcohol or vinegar. These drops are directly inserted into the mouth with a dropper. Tinctures are more potent than teas, especially when extracting aromatic oils and resins from the plant and barks. Tinctures can come in liquid, tablet, caplet, capsule form as well as in liquid form.

Tinctures are very popular among people because they do not require big preparation time and provide noticeable effects within minutes after application.

Tinctures can be used to treat many symptoms of different diseases, such as indigestion, stomach aches, sugar disorders or headaches.

Vinegar can be used to make tinctures; vinegar is an essential part of herbal medicine and it is usually used in making tinctures.

Tinctures are important at home, especially for first aid because they contain the most potent herbs in just a few drops. Tinctures are easy to travel with because they are in liquid form and do not take up too much space.

Find a list of herbs below that can be used to create different tinctures for various purposes.

Indigestion Tincture

Preparation:

Add one tablespoon of dried mint leaves to one-half cup of water in a pot.

Bring it to a boil, turn off the stove, and let it steep and cool down for about 10 minutes.

Line the alembic with cheesecloth and then add mint mixture through it into your bottle of choice.

Now, screw the cap on firmly and store it in a cool and dark place for at least 2 weeks.

Take 2 spoonfuls of tincture into the mouth, swish it around to spread it evenly on your teeth, gums and other parts of the mouth.

After that, you can take more tinctures as required depending on how well you feel after the first application.

You can also add Tincture to your food or juices.

Unlock Bactericidal Properties

Cough and Cold Tincture

Preparation:

Mix one tablespoon of chamomile with one cup of water in a pot.

Boil the mixture for about five minutes and then cover it until it is cooled for at least ten minutes.

Use 2-3 drops of tincture as needed for cough or cold.

Unlock Anti-inflammatory Properties

Painkiller Tincture

Preparation:

Mix one tablespoon of chamomile with two cups of water in a pot.

Boil the mixture for about five minutes and then cover it until it is cooled for at least ten minutes.

Use 2-3 drops of tincture as needed for headache, cramps, or other types of pain.

Infusion

An infusion is prepared by mixing the herbs with water or oil and waiting for the chemical compounds to mix with the solvent. This process is known as steeping. Infusion is used to make herbal remedies. The advantage of infusion is that it is easy to prepare and has the strong medicinal quality of the herb.

A very small number of herbs can be used for infusion because they are made up of many herbs, which results in a very mild flavor. Herbal tea or herbal soup is made through the process of infusions.

One can brew an infusion by placing herbs in a jug with clean water and placing it in sunlight for several hours, usually six to ten hours, depending on the herb type. When the water has reached full flavor, it can be drunk at once or have a second steep.

Infusions can be used to address all symptoms of illness and can also be used at any time when needed. It is an excellent way of treating mild problems and preventing disease symptoms and serious disorders by drinking herbal tea three times a day. Herbal teas are made by infusing herbs in boiling water for a few minutes and removing the mixture before drinking it.

Many of the materials used are leaves, flowers, berries, and seeds either in whole or dried and pounded or ground. The liquid is boiled and the herbs are added and allowed to steep for some time, usually 15-30 minutes. The herbs can be removed, or the liquid is strained and drunk either immediately or later.

Here is a list of herbs Infusions can be made with.

Sore Throat Infusion

Preparation:

Pour two cups of water into a pot, add one teaspoon of fresh ginger and bring it to a boil.

Turn off the stove and let it steep for 10 minutes.

Use 1-2 teaspoons of the mixture as often as needed for sore throat pain relief.

People who regularly take this infusion have fewer cases of the sore throat every year because they have strong bacterial resistance.

Infusion of Sage

Preparation:

Pour two cups of water into a pot, add one ounce of sage leaves and bring it to a boil.

Please turn off the stove and let it steep for 10 minutes.

Use 2-4 teaspoons of the mixture as often as needed for chest colds.

People who regularly take this infusion have fewer cases of the sore throat every year because they have strong bacterial resistance.

Infusion of Fennel

Preparation:

Pour two cups of water into a pot, add one teaspoon of fennel leaves and bring it to a boil.

Turn off the stove and let it steep for 10 minutes.

Use 1-2 teaspoons of the mixture as often as needed for cold, cough and respiratory disorders.

People who regularly take this infusion have fewer cases of constipation every year because they have strong bacterial resistance.

Infusion of Valerian

Preparation:

Pour two cups of water into a pot, add one teaspoon of fresh parsley flowers and bring it to a boil.

Turn off the stove and let it steep for 10 minutes.

Use 2-4 teaspoons with ½ teaspoon of valerian root as needed for insomnia, anxiety and nervousness.

People who regularly take this infusion have fewer cases of insomnia every year because they have strong bacterial resistance.

Infusion of Mint Tea

Preparation:

Pour two cups of water into a pot, add one teaspoon of fresh mint leaves and bring it to a boil.

Turn off the stove and let it steep for 10 minutes.

Use 1-2 teaspoons with ½ teaspoon of ginger as needed for stomach aches, nausea and vomiting.

People who regularly take this infusion have fewer cases of stomach aches every year because they have strong bacterial resistance.

Infusion of Licorice Tea

Preparation:

Pour two cups of water into a pot, add one teaspoon of dried licorice root and bring it to a boil.

Turn off the stove and let it steep for 10 minutes.

Use 1-2 teaspoons with ½ teaspoon of fenugreek as needed for cough, sore throat, flu and bronchitis.

People who regularly take this infusion have fewer cough cases every year because they have strong bacterial resistance.

Infusion of Unfermented Tea

Preparation:

Pour two cups of water into a pot, add one teaspoon of fresh mint leaves and bring it to a boil.

Turn off the stove and let it steep for 10 minutes.

Use 1-2 teaspoons with ½ teaspoon of chamomile as needed for indigestion, morning sickness, menstrual cramps and headaches.

People who regularly take this infusion have fewer cases of indigestion, morning sickness or headaches every year because they have strong bacterial resistance.

Infusion of Inflammatory Tea

Preparation:

Pour two cups of water into a pot, add one teaspoon of bergamot leaves and bring it to a boil.

Please turn off the stove and let it steep for 10 minutes.

Use 1-2 teaspoons with ½ teaspoon of ginger as needed for rheumatic problems and arthritis.

People who regularly take this infusion have fewer rheumatic problems every year because they have strong bacterial resistance.

Infusion of Yellow Dock Tea

Preparation:

Pour two cups of water into a pot, add one teaspoon of fresh dandelion and bring it to a boil.

Turn off the stove and let it steep for 10 minutes.

Use 1-2 teaspoons as needed for liver disorders, skin problems and urinary tract infections.

People who regularly take this infusion have fewer liver disorders and skin problems every year because they have strong bacterial resistance.

Infusion of Dandelion Tea

Preparation:

Pour two cups of water into a pot, add one teaspoon of fresh dandelion leaves and bring it to a boil.

Turn off the stove and let it steep for 10 minutes.

Use 1-2 teaspoons as needed for liver disorders, skin problems and urinary tract infections.

People who regularly take this infusion have fewer liver disorders and skin problems every year because of strong bacterial resistance.

Infusion of Bitter Tea

Preparation:

Pour two cups of water into a pot, add one teaspoon of fresh mint leaves and bring it to a boil.

Please turn off the stove and let it steep for 10 minutes.

Use 1-2 teaspoons as needed to lose appetite, colic, nausea, morning sickness and indigestion.

People who regularly take this infusion have a fewer loss of appetite, colic and morning sickness every year because they have a strong bacterial resistance.

Conclusion

Herbal medicine can be an effective part of treating various diseases and ailments. It is the most cost-effective form of medicine since it does not involve doctors or medicines. There are several different forms of herbal remedies used to treat many medical conditions, especially the ones that involve the body's internal organs such as the nervous system, digestions, heart, lungs, and immune system.

The most important thing to remember is that every herb has serious medicinal properties which can solve symptoms that may be causing disease or illness. Thus, it is essential to know the dosage of herbal remedies used in a recipe. Most are used in several forms, such as tinctures, infusions, and teas. It is easy to use them by placing them in the mouth or rubbing them on the skin.

Herbs can be used alone or mixed with other herbs because many herbs have different medicinal properties that activate more than one body's physiological function. For example, an herb contains anti-inflammatory properties, antioxidant, anti-microbial, and anti-tumor effects. Thus, an infusion of a single herb can be used to treat several symptoms of disease and protect organs.

I hope these four books have explained everything that you wanted to know about Native American Herb Medicine. There are many books that you can buy online or in bookstores. These books will help you understand more about taking care of yourself and preventing disease and treating any illness that you may have.

I would also like to thank all the readers who have read these books and I hope that I have given you the best information about natural medicine and health supplements.